THE MESSAGE OF FILM 6

Jesus in Modern Media

A Family Thing
Air Force One
Contact
Courage Under Fire
Dead Man Walking
Jurassic Park
Romeo and Juliet
Shine
Sleepers
Speed 2: Cruise Control
Star Trek: First Contact
The Great Santini
The Lost World
The Man Without A Face
The Spitfire Grill
Volcano

Michael Scully, OFM Cap.

Editors: Lynn Bruce
          Jean Finch
          Mary Winter

> To those who gave me time to write:
> Administrative Assistants:
> Cyndy Dreiling
> Cheryl Glassman
> Sandy Losey
>
> To the young people
> who teach me

HI-TIME Publishing
330 Progress Road
Dayton, OH 45449
800-558-2292   FAX 800-370-4450

© 1999 Michael Scully, OFM Cap., and HI-TIME Publishing

All rights reserved. No part of this book may be reproduced or transmitted in any form or by any means, electronic or mechanical, including photo-copying, recording or by an information storage and retrieval system without permission in writing from the publisher.

ISBN 0-937997-44-7

CONTENTS

Preface 1
General Introduction 1 5
General Introduction 2 9

    A Family Thing 13
    Air Force One 21
    Contact 31
    Courage Under Fire 43
    Dead Man Walking 53
    Jurassic Park 63
    Romeo and Juliet 71
    Shine 81
    Sleepers 89
    Speed 2: Cruise Control 101
    Star Trek: First Contact 109
    The Great Santini 117
    The Lost World 127
    The Man Without A Face 137
    The Spitfire Grill 147
    Volcano 157

Index of Scripture Passages 167
Index of Themes 169

PREFACE

I am more and more amazed at how movies speak to us. In particular, I was amazed at how the movies of this volume of *The Message of Film* spoke to me. I may be getting sentimental in my older age or maybe a little more concerned when I see how people react to certain situations, but I found myself very much affected by the movies which are presented here.

Maybe you would be interested in the way I first felt about the films since it might be a way for you to judge whether you would want to use the film either in class or for personal enrichment.

Before I go into them, however, a word or two about the use of movies in valuable class time. I know I address this in the general introduction, but since last year, I have received some criticism with the use of movies, and I wanted to reflect a little here. In particular, the accusation was made that I was "dumbing down religion" by showing films. I'm sure that was part of the reason why I added the numbers of the *Catechism* to each session of each movie. But, also, I feel once again compelled to defend the use of an occasional film (or more) in a religion class. Generally speaking, the goal of what the movie wanted to accomplish can only be achieved after the complete movie has been viewed. Because I like to spend quality time in class, I have often wished that I could acquire the feeling that a movie gives without showing the complete movie. But I don't think it is possible. Every once in a while, a point can be made with a short section of some movie, but I know that the full effect of the general theme of the movie can only come after its complete showing. I believe that the time is well spent because of the teaching that the movie brings.

I don't think I have ever felt the way I did after seeing the movies *Shine, Sleepers* and *The Great Santini*. What we do to young people is absolutely incredible. I know I wanted to get into the situation of the movie and change some things. I wanted to talk to the parents of these young people, and beg them to understand what they were doing. I wanted to stop the adult people who were misleading the kids and young people in the films. It was so frustrating to watch what is so predictable when adults do not know what they are doing to the young. *Of course*, the kids turned out the way they did. Look at what we adults and parents do—or don't do. The movies hurt me almost personally, and reinforced my desire to teach and say good things to our kids, trying, at least as far as I can, to tell them how important they are.

I wanted to include both *Jurassic Park* and *The Lost World* in this volume because most every young person has either seen one or both of them, or they have heard about them, and may even have formed some opinions as a result of them. The feeling I had initially as I prepared them was one of awe at the technology, but I also felt disgust at

PREFACE

how we will use anyone and anything to get money. Money is absolutely the root of all evil, and it is clearly portrayed in both of the films.

I wanted to include movies that were extremely popular, and which had a lot of action. My thinking was that young people go to these shows quite often and don't really think about any moral implications. Therefore, my feeling was that if I "write them up" with a moral thought in mind, I might be able to give you, their teachers, the opportunity to do the same. Consequently, you will see some "unlikely" teaching films in this series. **Air Force One** presents a unique opportunity to talk about people whom we consider evil, but who are just as devoted to their own beliefs as we are. I really like the chance to talk about the scene where Ivan the terrorist tells Alice, the daughter of President Marshall, that her father is exactly like him. In **Speed 2: Cruise Control**, I like the idea of never giving up, even in the face of one difficulty after another. There were many times during the movie when I found myself thinking "Now, how are they going to get out of this one!" **Star Trek: First Contact** gave me the opportunity to treat evil once again, somewhat the way I treated it in the last volume of **The Message of Film** in the *Star Wars Trilogy*. I must also admit that I am somewhat of a "trekky" and have always wanted to see if I could "work up" some morality thoughts about either set of Star Treks which I have enjoyed over the years. Finally, **Volcano** gave me the opportunity to talk about one of the highest tragedies we can think of in which thousands could be killed with seemingly no way out. I think we need to stretch our morality to see what we would do should such a thing ever happen. I especially liked the choice which Mike faced between saving his family or saving the general public.

I believe that family is of extreme importance in today's world, especially for our young people. Although there are many examples of good (and bad) family settings throughout the movies of the book, the one that I believe speaks it best is the movie **A Family Thing**. The feeling that struck me as I worked on it was how uncomfortable the movie made me feel. How strong is the feeling of prejudice in our society? It is a question which can be brought out very well as people study Raymond and Earl, and how they interacted in the movie.

I loved working on **Romeo and Juliet** because of the challenge. Shakespearean language is not the easiest language in the world to understand, but the modern version of the movie is done beautifully with young stars whom your students know immediately. I wanted to get into the movie as best I could, which led to my re-reading of Shakespeare's play and comparing the movie with the play. You can see it in the treatment of the movie in the book. I have placed the corresponding part of the play in the proper session of the movie, and I remember thinking how close the movie was to the play, and what an interesting concept the production was. It also fit very well into a marriage course which I am teaching to high school seniors. I especially found it

PREFACE

refreshing (the word I used in the commentary) to see that the young people (especially Juliet) wanted to be sure to be married before they experienced sex.

I have always had the highest respect for the intelligence of real life scientists. And I have always had the highest regard for the scientists who disagree with many of their colleagues by actually accepting God into their "scientific approach." I am very proud to be a friend of a geologist at Kansas University who is retired now, but who began his Geology 101 course with the statement that he was both a scientist and a Benedictine Oblate who accepted Jesus Christ as Lord. One can easily see, then, my regard for the movie *Contact*. I use the movie as a final movie before high school seniors graduate into the world, pointing out to them the importance of faith even as they live in an often faith-less world.

Finally, I think we have been blessed with some excellent examples of role models in the movies of this last year. I wanted to try to capture them with the use of four movies in particular. The final scene of *Courage Under Fire* still affects me even though I have studied it several times. It is truly a moving experience, and I remember thinking how crucial the "truth" is in life, and often we do not act like it. The movie *Dead Man Walking* is probably among the best ten movies I have ever studied, because of how real it is, and how difficult life is, especially in the face of tragedies. Sr. Helen Prejean, C.S.J. is a role model that everyone of us could easily study and imitate. Again, the idea of "truth" was paramount in my mind as I studied the movie. Justin McLeod is one of the most honorable men I have ever studied, as he is portrayed in *The Man Without a Face*, and one that can be a tutor to us as he was to young Charles Norstadt. And finally, what may be the best movie in this volume, although even as I write such a sentence I know I could argue with myself. Let's say it was a movie that had a profound effect on me, and probably will every time I see it, *The Spitfire Grill*. I think it is so important for young people to see other young people who, even though they are very sincere, are misjudged by those around them. I think the scene with Percy Talbot and Eli is among the most touching moments I have ever seen on film.

These are some of my thoughts as I have worked with the sixteen movies of this volume of *The Message of Film*. I know that I learned a number of things about myself as I worked with them; I trust the same will happen to you and/or your students. But, most of all, I believe these movies will give our young people the chance to understand that the movies they watch may indeed be entertaining, but they also can teach valuable lessons. They are lessons that could literally save our souls.

                                                Michael Scully
                                                April, 1998
                                                Hays, Kansas

GENERAL INTRODUCTION 1

The Use of Popular Films in Youth Ministry

One of the most interesting documents resulting from the Second Vatican Council was the document entitled *Gaudium et Spes*, or as it has come to be known, the "Pastoral Constitution of the Church in the Modern World." Interestingly, this document was not even imagined at the beginning of the Council. The Council Fathers themselves chose to address the subject of the "world and modern people."[1] Never before had an official document looked at the subject in quite the same way. It did not condemn. It only reflected and offered pastoral statements.

One such statement could be applied to modern media. The Council Fathers wrote in their introductory statement: "The Church as always has the duty of scrutinizing the signs of the times and of interpreting them in the light of the Gospel. Thus, in language intelligible to each generation, she can respond to the perennial questions which ask about this present life and the life to come, and about the relationship of the one to the other. We must therefore recognize and understand the world in which we live, its expectations, its longings, and its often dramatic characteristics."[2]

As we "recognize and understand the world in which we live," especially in the arena of youth activity, we must encounter the motion picture, one of the major, if not *the* major form of entertainment for American youth. Therefore the "duty" for the Church, and therefore the religious educator, is to "scrutinize" the motion picture and interpret it in the "light of the Gospel."

There are many ways of going about that task. Many choose to take a negative route declaring that the modern film has nothing significant to offer in light of the Gospel. I think such an approach is neither profitable, nor true. Every modern film has a message, even if it is totally inane, and since the Scriptures talk about life and every form of life in one way or another, there is the possibility of teaming up some specific Scripture passages with the message of the film. Such is the approach of this resource book.

This book, as well as the other books of the series *Jesus in Modern Media*,[3] emphasizes that modern media is a means to teach our junior high, senior high, and college youth. It is a method that uses the actual media without alteration and then simply scrutinizes it in light of the Gospel.

GENERAL INTRODUCTION 1

I feel that such an approach is not only useful, but it is absolutely necessary given the young person of today. A critic in one of the nation's leading media magazines, *Variety*, wrote already in 1985, "While TV networks, radio programs, the music world, magazines, and the video world cater to the young, the strongest attempt to win the minds and souls of young people probably occurs in the film industry."[4] The language of the critic is interesting: it is an "attempt to win the minds and souls of young people." Should not the Church, then, in scrutinizing the signs of the times, address this medium of entertainment with the intention of "using" what it has to offer in light of the Gospel?

Hundreds of films are produced every year. Although all of them can be scrutinized, and perhaps should be scrutinized, in light of the Gospel, there are many that would fall into the category of what I refer to as "teaching films," that is, films with a message that can serve as a teacher for everyone including the young person. These are the films which are the subject of this book. The movies I have chosen, I believe, make a significant statement to young people in particular.

We are in difficult times in the field of religious education. Most of us do not work out of a Catholic school setting on a junior high, senior high, or college level. We do not have the opportunity every day or every other day of teaching the young people we so desperately want to educate. We have them at most once a week. How do we give quality education on a subject that is so important, if not the most important subject of their lives--religion--given those time constraints? It is the essential question for parochial religious education.

This book is my contribution to a solution. The idea is a simple one. Take the popular films that most every teenager has already seen and apply them to different parts of Scripture, showing how Scripture has "something to say" in the same area that the film is considering. The movies for this volume are recent releases and some of them have been honored with an award from the motion picture industry. Consequently, they would qualify as "good" in one way or another.

The content of the course is necessarily supplied by the movie itself, but the general themes of the movies can easily be arranged in such a way as to either provide the sole content of a year-long course or as a supplement for part of a course. Most major concerns of a young person and the religious educator's desire for a Christian

GENERAL INTRODUCTION 1

understanding of them are illustrated by the movies contained in this and every volume of *The Message of Film*.

Consequently, I believe that this is a good way to educate our youth. Furthermore, I would go so far as to say that it is an essential way. My reasons are as follows:

1. As explained above, movies are "where they are." The average American teenager is viewing at least one movie a week either in the movie theater or through the VCR. Therefore the film exercises an incredible amount of power in speaking to teenagers.

2. Obviously, this is a way of gaining their attention. Young people almost always "get into" films. They will fix themselves on the images of a movie screen much more easily than they will on an instructor, no matter how good the course is. Religious educators always understand that they are "competing" with real professionals when it comes to "gaining attention." Young people are constantly exposed to the highest quality presentations in theaters, on television, and radio: what religious educators can do by themselves is often mediocre. Why not use the talents of those who make excellent films?

3. The young person will know the film, especially if it is one that appeals to the younger ages, and therefore a significant part of a lesson to be taught is "automatic": namely, knowledge of the situation. The educator must supply the "morality content," but it will not be an especially difficult task since knowledge of the situation is a "given."

4. Almost every good film--and certainly every film included in this volume--has some type of a God-figure or Jesus-figure. The realization that even the modern secular film contains images of the types of people religious educators want young people to be has a powerful impact on the young mind.

5. Every educator has experienced the inability to convey some particular concept well. It is often much easier to refer to a film which "says" it for us. The film portrays the concept and provides the opportunity to discuss that concept as it is portrayed.

6. It is a well-known axiom that a picture is worth a thousand words. An idea portrayed on the screen has much greater impact than an instructor's vocal presentation.

GENERAL INTRODUCTION 1

7. Movies often have many themes running through them, and frequently one of the "minor themes" is one that strikes a young person. Such a topic may not be "covered" in a regular religion class.

8. Almost every film contains some type of violence or sexual activity. These topics must be addressed for the modern teen and a good film will usually provide the opportunity of discussing the topics directly and in a setting that "makes sense" to the young person. [Note: I do not feel that the "porno film" or X-rated movies supply this opportunity since most of the time the intention of the film maker is much less noble.]

9. Using films "in the classroom" promotes the idea that "not everything in the media is bad." Too often we jump to a negative conclusion about the media which is not warranted. Adults must be convinced that there is good in the media; our discussion of a film in a class with their kids may help to produce a more positive image of the media.

10. Perhaps most importantly, movies tend to promote participation. Young people may have a difficult time talking about their individual problems, but it is relatively easy for them to talk about other people's problems that resemble theirs. Working with films supplies such an opportunity.

I hope you find this resource book helpful not only because I want to sell books, but also because I want to sell "the idea." Our youth need direction. Many of them are not coming to the very class that can give such direction--the religious education class. I believe the films in this book can attract an audience and, at the same time, they can enable the religious educator to get inside the minds and souls of young people at a time when "religion" must be there.

Footnotes:
1. *Pastoral Constitution of the Church in the Modern World.* Abbott, Walter M., S.J., ed. *The Documents of Vatican II.* New York: Guild Press, p. 200.
2. Ibid., p. 201-202.
3. Present available volumes:
   The Message of Film 4, The Message of Rock 95-96, The Message of Film 5, The Message of Rock 1997.
4. As quoted in Schultze, Quentin J., project coordinator. *Dancing in the Dark.* Grand Rapids, MI: William B. Erdmans Publishing, p. 211.

GENERAL INTRODUCTION 2

A Method of Using the Films Presented in This Book

There is no doubt in my mind, as you have seen from my previous introduction, that popular films should be used in youth ministry. In my own high school religious education courses, I have gone to almost exclusive use of media--music, rock videos, television, commercials, films--working with them "in light of the Gospel." So I come to you with this approach as "field tested." The young people with whom I have had the privilege of working seem to "buy into" this approach to religious education rather well.

How do I suggest that you, as a youth minister, use this material to teach religious education? First of all, I think it must be said that this material could be used for personal growth, even though it is not written with that in mind. Making use of this material as "personal meditation," I believe, will enable one not only to enjoy the movie, but also to grow spiritually. But the main purpose of this material is for teaching junior high, senior high, and college youth.

May I say some things about "time" first. If you are a teacher of students whom you have the opportunity to see every day or every other day in your class, I would suggest you plan to spend a whole week or perhaps two on the material. There should be a significant amount of time, of personal reflection, written reports, and certainly quality discussion. As I teach religion every day, I find that four films a semester, spaced appropriately, is just about right.

Most of the youth ministers who will use this resource book, however, will only have one hour or one and a half hours a week. It is with this in mind that the material was written.

I believe you can profitably devote a whole year course to films. Choose four or five of the films for each semester according to what you believe should be presented to your young people. The *General Themes* written for each film give an overall idea of the content contained in the film, and you can easily arrange these to cover whatever areas you want.

Another way of using the films is, of course, to only use one or two to supplement the material that you are presenting. In that case, again, the *General Themes* will help you choose which films would best fit your plan. This book of *The Message of Film*

GENERAL INTRODUCTION 2

continues to place a thematic arrangement of the different themes of the movies at the close of the volume as a reference (see p. 169). I hope you find it helpful as you search for ways to enhance your presentations to your students.

This year I have added the reference numbers to the *Catechism of the Catholic Church*. I use the sections of the *Catechism* as a way to begin the presentation of a session. I think it is very important to show the "general teaching" of the Church with regard to some doctrine or virtue before it is acted out in a particular way in the movie. Use of the *Catechism* enables the instructor to state exactly what the teaching of the Church is (and gives an opportunity to "test" the students' knowledge as well), and the movie will present the acceptance or non-acceptance of the doctrine. Consequently, the instructor can critique the movie with the exact words of the Church's official doctrine.

A word of caution about the use of films with younger students. I would suggest that the less mature the student, the more you must do in order to "teach" with the film. The immature student will want to "enjoy only" and thus miss what the educator and what this book is trying to do.

Also, I have found it very helpful to invite other adults besides myself to take part in the presentation. They should not be asked to be the main presenters for the class, but they can be extremely helpful when it comes to discussion, providing the point of view of some other adult.

The actual format I suggest would be as follows:

Rent or purchase the video cassette of the film. Concentrate on one session at a time. Trying to give too much material at once loses the effect of deeper discussion. You may even want to extend the film over a longer time than I have suggested in the text to enable more discussion. You should preview the whole film, however, before you begin the first presentation since it is good for you to know what is coming. But I strongly recommend that the teacher not give away the plot in case the students have not seen the film or have forgotten it. I have tried to write the *Preliminary Thought* questions with that in mind.

The actual class itself might begin with some quiet time, emphasizing that God is very much a part of the presentation, even though it is a secular film. Then either a student or adult should read the *Scripture* with some quiet time after it to allow it to make an impact. Then the *Doctrine/Application* meditation in the book should be read. You may want to amplify it yourself. I have tried to give whatever "doctrine" that

GENERAL INTRODUCTION 2

must be covered in the meditation, especially with the addition of the references to the *Catechism*, but you are better qualified to talk to your particular group.

After your presentation of the *Doctrine/Application* from the book and any personal reflection you might have, read one or more of the *Preliminary Thought* questions to the students. [Note: as with all the textbooks in this *Jesus in Modern Media* series, multiple buying of books is not necessary.] Give the students a few minutes so that they can formulate their own answers. You might want them to have paper and pencil for this portion. Also you may want to use other questions (and keep them in the space marked *Notes* in the book). Then perhaps a fifteen to twenty minute discussion could occur. The discussion will easily lead into the presentation of the film. You might want to summarize both what you want your students to look for in the session they will be watching as well as review the story line of the film, up to that point. Perhaps some questions can be taken at this time also.

Use the portion of the film suggested in the book. You might want to rewind it to catch a previous scene as you begin, but try to stop it exactly where the book suggests. I would also recommend that you *not* instruct during the film since it might interrupt the train of thought for the young people. After the actual presentation, I would suggest the following technique.

You might break up into small groups of five or six to a group, or simply remain as a large group depending on the size of your class. Ask the students to take about two or three minutes of silence and either write down or arrange their thoughts in answer to the question, "What scene during the session strikes you the most and why?" This is where I have had some good discussion. Then, if you have time--and my guess is that there will not be much left--you might want to go into the questions and remarks of the *Reflection/Ideas/Discussion* section from the book.

This is how I have taught with these films. It is the method that has worked for me, but individual teachers are not only encouraged to go their own direction, but should look on it as a duty to come up with their own individual ways of presenting the material.

A note here, as I have made in the other books of this series. This book is meant to "put me out of business." You can easily see how I have worked with these films. There may be films that you as the teacher want to present using the same method. I encourage you to do just that.

GENERAL INTRODUCTION 2

I hope you *can* use this resource book. And I hope you do. As religious educators, we must reach the level of the young people in order to teach them what they need. Used well, I believe this will do it!

A FAMILY THING

GENERAL THEME

An important part of maturity is getting to know one's family.

SESSION I
From: Begins right away.
To: After Ray says, "I ain't worried about it."
Approximate time: 36 minutes.

Theme: Prejudice can cease only when we truly understand others and their situations.

Scripture: **Acts 15:6-12** Peter urges his fellow disciples to learn tolerance.

Doctrine/Application
[*Catechism of the Catholic Church* **reference:** numbers 2477-2478]

The beginning of the Christian community was not without difficulty. Their founder had preached love and harmony and above all, a certain universal equality. No one was to be better than anyone else. It seems strange then that the problem that came close to destroying the early community was prejudice. In fact, the moment of history which Christians named the Council of Jerusalem was convened for the primary reason of establishing true equality. Realizing that prejudice can cease only when there is true understanding of everyone's situation, Peter implored his fellow disciples to make no distinction between the believing Jews and Gentiles. In his words, one can easily hear Peter suggest that the early Christians should know each other better so that together they could find the real equality that Jesus wanted.

Equality of people is still a problem among Christians, indeed among all nations. In North America, black Americans have continually struggled with a prejudice against them that dates back centuries. Equality of peoples still does not come easily, especially in the southern United States, especially also in families where black and white work closely together. Such is the setting of the movie "A Family Thing."

There is much to learn from Earl Pilcher and Raymond Murdock. One can learn from the uneasiness that comes from unexpected discoveries. One can learn from the anger which comes against parents who no longer remember the exploits of their early years. One can especially learn from the difficulties each of them has as they deal with a closeness to each other that they would prefer to avoid.

A FAMILY THING

Christianity began by fighting prejudice. Christianity must continue to fight it in our present day before we can truly learn about Jesus' ways.

Preliminary Thought

1. Define "prejudice" as you understand it.
2. Give some instances of prejudice that you see a) in your nation, b) in your community, c) in your family.
3. Do you believe that every member of the Christian church is treated in an equal way? Yes or no and why?
4. Practically, what can be done by young people to promote the fight against racial prejudice?

Notes

Reflection/Ideas/Discussion

WHAT SCENE DURING THIS SESSION STRIKES YOU THE MOST AND WHY?

5. Scene analysis: Earl's mother is dying. The death of a parent is among the most difficult situations a human being must face. In what way does a Christian's understanding of the death of a parent differ from a non-believer's understanding? Explain your answer.
6. Character analysis: Earl's father. Granted that we know little about him from the movie, but judging from the way he is presented so far, discuss his character.

A FAMILY THING

> 7. Scene analysis: Earl is upset when he discovers the identity of his real mother. Do you think that such a discovery should make a real difference in a person's life? Yes or no and why?
> 8. Scene analysis: Earl's family at the meal. Earl evidently is disturbed and "takes it out" on his family. What is the best way for others to act when one family member is as disturbed as Earl was? Explain your answer.
> 9. Dialogue analysis: Raymond asks Earl how it feels to be "colored." Describe your feeling if you suddenly found out that you had a brother that was a different race from you.
> 10. Scene analysis: Earl is mugged and robbed. a) What is the principal cause for such happenings in our larger cities? b) What are some ways to prevent it from happening?
> 11. Scene analysis: Raymond takes Earl to Raymond's home. Do you think *most* people would have behaved the way Raymond did? Yes or no and why?

Notes

SESSION II

From: After Ray says, "I ain't worried about it."
To: After Virgil says to his kids: "No, you can't watch TV; I'm turning the lights out."
Approximate time: 35 minutes.

Theme: In order to feel satisfied in life, one must truly understand one's immediate family.

Scripture: **Matthew 2:19-23** Joseph makes some decisions concerning family life.

A FAMILY THING

Doctrine/Application
[*Catechism of the Catholic Church* reference: numbers 2204-2206]

Jesus began his life with very special circumstances. One can easily imagine Joseph and Mary pulling Jesus aside later on in life and telling him exactly what went on. Their words, of course, are not recorded, but one could guess that they resembled Aunt T's words to Earl in the movie, "A Family Thing." She said to him, "You need to know your history, son." As Jesus Christ had to be aware of his history with all its intrigue in order to know himself better, so Earl had to learn about his brother Ray and his family to have a better knowledge of just who he was.

One of the great lessons in life is what we learn from and about our own families. Most of us experience normal enough family lives as we grow. There are the good times and the bad times, the closeness and the fights, the big events that we look forward to with joy and the day-to-day drudgery. Most of us do not understand that we are always learning, and always developing a personality that will be unique. Through it all, we are establishing a foundation that will last for a long time.

As Earl does in the movie "A Family Thing," as Jesus no doubt did during his early years, we all should study our family patterns and our own contribution to them. Many times deep friendships form from early family living, but unfortunately we all know of deep hatred that also arises. This session of "A Family Thing" might provide an opportunity to study the type of patterns that are forming with our families right now.

Preliminary Thought

12. [The instructor may want to plan some silence for this exercise.] a) Take some time to carefully consider the relationship with each of your immediate family, asking what kind of a relationship you have, placing each one on a scale of 1-5 where 5 is high. b) After the exercise, determine how you can make your relationship with each member any better.
13. Families are labeled dysfunctional when something is seriously wrong with the family patterns. If you were a family counselor, what would be the characteristics that you would stress that every family should possess.

A FAMILY THING

Notes

Reflection/Ideas/Discussion

WHAT SCENE DURING THIS SESSION STRIKES YOU THE MOST AND WHY?

14. Scene analysis: Do you think that Virgil had a right to know about the invitation to Earl to stay at Ray's house? Yes or no and why?

15. Dialogue/scene analysis: Evidently his father has lectured Virgil many times about the responsibility of raising children. In your opinion, what are the most important characteristics that should be present as parents raise children?

16. Dialogue analysis: Aunt T tells Earl that he can't help how he was born. It is a true statement, obviously, but if parents know that there were "special circumstances" when a child is born, for example, conception before the marriage or a different father, do you think that they should tell their children? Yes or no and why?

17. Dialogue analysis: Aunt T tells Earl that nobody ever knows what it's like for somebody else. We tend to judge others by how we feel. Why did Jesus talk against judging others?

18. Dialogue analysis: Virgil talks to his Dad and Aunt T about Earl's presence in the home. When we talk ill of others, it can easily get back to them. What is a general Christian rule concerning talking to other people?

19. Scene analysis: Ray and Earl fight. Watching the two older men physically fight calls to mind the stupidity of physical confrontations. Do you believe that there is ever a time when we should physically attack someone else? Yes or no and why?

A FAMILY THING

> 20. Dialogue analysis: Earl did not mean his statement that he wasn't afraid of Ray or any other "nigger on the street." a) Why did he say it? b) How did Ray "hear" it? c) Should Ray have been so upset? Yes or no and why?
> 21. Dialogue analysis: Aunt T tells Ray to overcome his pride. Why are we so proud that we will not admit fault?
> 22. Scene analysis: Earl at the bar, celebrating the birthday party, and dancing with the young lady. In your opinion, what lesson did director Richard Pearce want to accomplish with this scene?
> 23. Scene analysis: As Ray looks for Earl, he is held at gun point, but nothing happens. Is there some lesson of this scene also? Yes or no and why?
> 24. Dialogue analysis: Earl says that he didn't think he would wake up and it has made him feel thankful. Do you believe that we are thankful enough for the simple things we have? Yes or no and why?
> 25. Scene analysis: The picnic in the park. Obviously, Virgil and Ann have severe difficulties communicating with each other. If you were a counselor and they wanted help, what would you suggest first?

Notes

SESSION III

From: After Virgil says to his kids: "No, you can't watch TV; I'm turning the lights out."

To: End.

Approximate time: 36 minutes.

Theme: Family members can be friends with each other only when they are giving to each other.

A FAMILY THING

Scripture: **Matthew 7:12-14** Jesus' presents his doctrine concerning the Golden Rule and the narrow gate.

Doctrine/Application
[*Catechism of the Catholic Church* **reference:** number 2207]

The recently discovered blood brothers Earl Pilcher and Raymond Murdock in the movie "A Family Thing" knew the meaning of the narrow gate of the Sermon on the Mount. It was the gate that those who accepted the golden rule could enter even if it were narrow. Focused on the idea of doing things on behalf of others, one learns the value of true giving. Earl and Ray during this final segment develop the ability to truly give to one another. In the process, they not only realize their bloodline, but they become friends as well.

During the second session of the movie, Ray and Earl had begun to understand each other. Now, as they begin to truly love each other, they provide further inspiration to the family members of our world. Their desire to give to each other is an example of what can hold a family together, as well as the catalyst which produces strong caring personalities for later on in life. If family members want to be friends even as they remain closely related, the art of giving must be made a practical priority as they live together.

Giving, of course, is a general virtue that must have many daily practical conclusions. And some days the family is better at giving to each other than other days. But if a family can enter the narrow gate of giving and doing on behalf of the others in the family, the road to happiness will be theirs. It is a happiness that not only encompasses their daily living as they grow. It will also produce a life of giving for each member after they have left the home.

Preliminary Thought

26. Every major religion accepts the golden rule. Do you believe it has made a major impact on the world? Yes or no and why?
27. Discuss some ways that family members can truly give to each other.
28. If we were a friend of someone who "hates" his brother or sister in their family, what are the ways that you could help the relationship?

A FAMILY THING

Notes

Reflection/Ideas/Discussion

WHAT SCENE DURING THIS SESSION STRIKES YOU THE MOST AND WHY?

29. Dialogue/scene analysis: Ray and Earl talk about Virgil's children being caught between the parents. Undoubtedly, this is the worst situation for children. Do you believe that divorced parents honestly consider what their divorce does to their children? Yes or no and why?

30. Dialogue/scene analysis: Ray says that a person can be saved if he/she wants to be saved. True or false and why?

31. Dialogue/scene analysis: Earl talks to Virgil. a) Why didn't Virgil want to listen to what Earl had to say? b) Earl's definition of happiness: "Nothing more than having something to look forward to." Why is this a good definition of happiness? c) Earl says that he and Virgil have in common the fact that there is something they both *have* to do. As you generalize the statement, what does everyone really *have* to do?

32. Dialogue/scene analysis: Ray tells Earl that he hated Earl's dad. Ray felt that he had to say it. Why is it better to always get your serious feelings out in the open?

33. Dialogue/scene analysis: Aunt T tells the story of Earl's birth. What struck you the most about the story and why?

34. Scene analysis: Ray decides to go with Earl back to Arkansas. What do you think this action "said" to Earl?

35. Scene analysis: Ray and Earl drink a toast to their mother. a) What does the idea of a toast mean for people? b) Specifically, here, what did Ray and Earl mean to convey with the toast?

36. What message to North America does the movie "A Family Thing" present?

Further Material

AIR FORCE ONE

[This movie has been rated R by the motion picture industry because of violence.]

GENERAL THEME

As long as people believe in a cause, they can do harm unless they are ruled by morally correct principles.

SESSION I

From: Begins after the list of some of the credits (after credit listing: "Costume Designer: Erica Edith Phillips")
To: After the Vice-President says, "He had no right to take chances with his life."
Approximate time: 38 minutes.

Theme: Evil is defined differently depending on one's point of view. But it is always wrong.

Scripture: **John 19:4-11** The Hebrew people ask for Jesus' death.

Doctrine/Application
[*Catechism of the Catholic Church* **reference:** numbers 402-412]

The Christian would look at the death of Jesus to be one of the greatest evils that humankind has committed. But if the people who were shouting for Jesus' death were sincere—and we have no reason to think otherwise—there was no evil intention at all. Perhaps, they were merely desiring the removal of an impostor king who had misled thousands of people. (John 19:4-11) Evil is defined differently depending on one's point of view.

But can one ever justify the killing of an innocent man? Even if Jesus were evil, could there not have been another way to correct him? The real human evil in Jesus' death may have been nothing more than the fact that an innocent man was actually put to death.

The evil committed in the movie "Air Force One" is defined differently depending on one's point of view. For the free world, certainly for the people of the United States, to take any plane by force, let alone Air Force One, threatening to kill and actually killing people, is evil. For the Russian nationalists, who took the plane by force, the capture of General Radek after the killing of his guards was also an evil.

As one views the beginning of the movie "Air Force One," one must be struck by the violence and the killing that takes place. It happens in the opening scene by the

AIR FORCE ONE

Americans; it continues through the story of the terrorists' take-over of the most protected plane in the world. Both sides thought they were doing good, both sides defined evil their own way, but perhaps the real evil was overlooked. When innocent people are killed, it is always evil, no matter who does it, or what the motive.

This meditation is not meant to justify the actions of terrorists, whether American or otherwise. It is meant to call into question the unnecessary killing of innocent people. It could be that our world has been forever infected by evil and the only way to attack it is to become more peaceful in our approach to others, both on an international level as well as a personal one.

Preliminary Thought

1. Define "evil" as best you can.
2. What is the greatest evil in the world?
3. Reading the closing paragraph of the meditation, one is led to question whether the common people of our world can do anything about the evils that infect their lives. Realistically, what can be done?

Notes

Reflections/Ideas/Discussion

WHAT SCENE DURING THIS SESSION STRIKES YOU THE MOST AND WHY?

AIR FORCE ONE

4. Dialogue analysis: The President's speech. a) He says, "Real peace is not just the absence of conflict; it is the presence of justice." In your opinion, have we ever achieved such peace in the world? Yes or no and why? b) He also speaks of what is "morally right." Do you believe that the ideal of what is "morally right" is strong in our politics? Yes or no and why?
5. Dialogue analysis: The President and his wife reminisce about the campaign, and talk about doing the right thing. As you study our political system and method of election, do you believe that our candidates are concerned about the right thing to do? Yes or no and why?
6. Scene analysis: The Chief of Secret Service kills the agents. What are the reasons a person so high in service to his government would do such a thing?
7. Scene analysis: The killings. They are graphically portrayed in the movie and the reason why the movie is rated R by the motion picture industry. Does such portrayal of violence in any way harm the people who are watching it? Yes or no and why?
8. Analysis: Alice, the President's daughter, twelve years old. Do you think that what she has seen will affect her in an adverse way in the future? Yes or no and why? [The instructor may want to ask this question in each session since Alice is an integral part in all the activity.]
9. Dialogue analysis: The terrorist Ivan explains that he wants Mother Russia to be a great nation again and have America beg for forgiveness. Referring to the meditation, his desire is not evil. How he brings it about is evil. Is killing really necessary to bring about what people think is good? Yes or no and why?
10. Dialogue analysis: One of the Vice-President's staff tells her that the terrorist is a zealot. Is there anything wrong with being a zealot? Yes or no and why?

Notes

AIR FORCE ONE

SESSION II

From: After the Vice-President says, "He had no right to take chances with his life."

To: After the Vice-President says, "Call the press room; we have to issue a statement. Walter, General."

Approximate time: 38 minutes.

Theme: When evil controls a situation, evil begets more evil and innocent people always get hurt.

Scripture: **Matthew 12:43-45** Evil begets evil.

Doctrine/Application
[*Catechism of the Catholic Church* **reference:** numbers 1707-1709]

It has been said that the first act of doing something morally wrong may be very difficult, but that each subsequent evil act is easier. Psychologically, the explanation probably lies in that doing something morally wrong will always bother a person's conscience. And since each act which follows will be easier on the conscience, we will offer less resistance.

In the language of Scripture, Jesus describes evil in terms of a devil occupying a person. "Then [the devil] goes and brings back with itself seven other spirits more evil than itself and they move in and dwell there; and the last condition of that person is worse than the first." (Matthew 12:45) Evil begets evil. Jesus was warning his disciples never to allow their guard to drop, nor to make the first step toward evil.

As one follows the activity during the second session of "Air Force One," one can see the principle which Jesus talked about at work in the mind of the terrorists, and in particular in the mind of their leader. Ivan will stop at nothing to get what he wants, and the means to get it gradually becomes more evil, and at the same time, for him, perhaps easier.

The people who are studying this movie to learn something of themselves will never commit the atrocities that are portrayed in the movie, but they have occasion to commit a significant amount of evil in their own circles of activity. The lesson of this session is a very straightforward one. It was the lesson of Jesus as he studied the evil in his world, an evil not too much different from ours. We cannot allow ourselves to begin to think in terms of evil, nor can we begin to act on it. If we do, it becomes even more difficult to stop. Evil is difficult at first; it is much easier as we involve ourselves in more of it.

AIR FORCE ONE

> **Preliminary Thought**
>
> 11. Study the evils which you think are part of the world right now. How do you see the principle of "evil begets evil" happening?
> 12. The meditation refers to evil in the common person. What are the most common evils which you see in your own world right now, and how do you see the principle of "evil begets evil" occurring?
> 13. Discuss how one stops the principle that "evil begets evil."

Notes

> **Reflections/Ideas/Discussion**
>
> **WHAT SCENE DURING THIS SESSION STRIKES YOU THE MOST AND WHY?**
> 14. Scene analysis: The Secretary of Defense and Vice-President argue about who is in charge. In your opinion, why did the argument take place?
> 15. Scene analysis: Ivan feels bad at the death of his comrade. We do not think in terms of a terrorist who has feelings for others. What should be our response at the death of someone close to us?
> 16. Scene analysis: The cold-blooded killing of the National Security Advisor (and later of Melanie). Is an execution such as this ever in order? Yes or no and why?
> 17. Dialogue/scene analysis: Ivan talks to Alice. a) "I have three small children." Does the fact that he is "a family man" fit into what you think a "terrorist" is? b) "Your father has also killed." True or false and why? c) Why did Ivan kiss Alice?

AIR FORCE ONE

> 18. Dialogue analysis: Explain the President and Vice-President's statement: "If you give a mouse a cookie, he is going to want a glass of milk." Discuss the truth of its meaning.
> 19. Dialogue analysis: Ivan says that they are at war. a) Is he correct? Yes or no and why? b) In your mind, define when a state of war exists.
> 20. Scene analysis: The Vice-President decides to re-fuel the plane. Was it a correct decision? Yes or no and why?

Notes

SESSION III

From: After the Vice-President says, "Call the press room; we have to issue a statement. Walter, General."
To: End.
Approximate time: 37 minutes.

Theme: The courageous person always considers the lives of others no matter what the circumstances.

Scripture: **Colossians 1:21-23**   Christ died for us to save us from our sins.

Doctrine/Application
[*Catechism of the Catholic Church* reference: number 1808]

It has been said, probably correctly, that the most powerful person in the world is the President of the United States. It may be that he is the most important person as well. At least, in the mind of most Americans, he has such a distinction. Therefore, from day one of his inauguration, the President is protected, and no matter what happens to anyone else, the President's security is the highest priority.

AIR FORCE ONE

President James Marshall was an extraordinary man. He had received the Medal of Honor for his bravery in Vietnam, and obviously from the movie so far, he is able to handle himself quite well despite uneven odds. But he is still the President. One would expect therefore that as things gradually turn toward the better, that the President would save himself, no matter what. Certainly, that is what everyone connected with him desired.

But, he doesn't. He wanted his family protected and he wanted the wounded, and even all of his staff taken care of before him. It is truly a courageous act, one in which President Marshall shows that he was willing to give up his life on behalf of others. To him, it was not courage, it was what should be.

When one talks of courage and the giving of oneself on behalf of others, the Christian must necessarily think of Jesus, the person whom Christians regard as Savior, the person who died for the sins of humankind. Paul discusses the fact with the Colossians: "And you who once were alienated and hostile in mind because of evil deeds," Paul writes, "he has now reconciled in his fleshly body through his death." (Colossians 1:21-22) In the Christian scheme of things, Jesus gave up his life on behalf of others.

We are not called to any significant act as Jesus was, or as President James Marshall was, but we are called to give on behalf of others. Jesus reminds us many times in the Scriptures that we are expected as his followers to give of ourselves on behalf of others. As we struggle in this world, everyone of us, Christian or not, must understand that the only way to lasting peace or just harmony is through the attitude of giving. Giving on behalf of others is not only the courageous thing to do; it could save our world.

Preliminary Thought

21. Do you think it is a good idea to have a "military person" be President of the United States or any country? Yes or no and why?
22. As you consider your life right now, what is the best way you can give to others?
23. Give an example of someone you know of who has given of his/her life for the sake of others.

AIR FORCE ONE

Notes

Reflection/Ideas/Discussion

WHAT SCENE DURING THIS SESSION STRIKES YOU THE MOST AND WHY?

24. Scene analysis: The Vice-President asks America to pray for the safety of the people on Air Force One. Does prayer play a *significant* part in the life of the American people? Yes or no and why?
25. Scene analysis: Ivan obviously has no respect for the President. Does he have cause to feel the way he does? Yes or no and why?
26. Scene analysis: The President cannot reason with Ivan concerning General Radek. Why is it so difficult to reason with terrorists?
27. Scene analysis: Should the President have allowed General Radek's release? Yes or no and why?
28. Scene analysis: The Secretary of Defense asks the Vice-President to sign the paper concerning the President's incompetence. What *should* she have done?
29. Scene analysis: Ivan's (and later on, the Chief of Staff's) death. There is some "relief," maybe even joy, at the death of the terrorists. Should we feel that way as Christians?
30. Scene analysis: One of the American pilots gave up his life to save Air Force One. Giving on behalf of others is what the meditation was about. Do you think that there are many such incidents of courage among the military of our country? Yes or no and why?
31. Scene analysis: The First Family hug. Do you think that most political "families" are this close? Yes or no and why?
32. What particular message should we learn from the movie "Air Force One"?

AIR FORCE ONE

Further Material

AIR FORCE ONE

CONTACT

GENERAL THEME

Science and technology should teach us that we are not alone in our universe because there is a Higher Power who has created it.

SESSION I
From: Begins immediately after title.
To: As Ellie is listening on the hood of her car, begins to hear a noise, and opens her eyes.
Approximate time: 36 minutes.

Theme: God is often misunderstood because we do not understand God.

Scripture: **Acts 17:22-28** Paul teaches about the true understanding of God.

Doctrine/Application
[*Catechism of the Catholic Church* reference: numbers 39-43]

The *Catechism of the Catholic Church*, quoting the fourth Lateran Council of the Church and St. Thomas Aquinas, states well the problem we have with understanding God: "We must recall that 'between Creator and creature no similitude can be expressed without implying an even greater dissimilitude'; and that 'concerning God, we cannot grasp what he is, but only what he is not, and how other beings stand in relation to him.'" (43) Paul the Apostle pointed out the same things to the Athenians at the Areopagus: "The God who made the world and all that is in it, the Lord of heaven and earth, does not dwell in sanctuaries made by human hands." (Acts 17:24) Both the *Catechism* and St. Paul speak of the difficulty of talking about God because we must use the human image.

And whenever we use the human image, not only do we not get a full picture, but we may very well introduce misunderstandings. Case in point: young Ellie Arroway in the movie "Contact." She lost her Mom and Dad when she was very young. To her young human mind, that should not have happened, and therefore a God who wants to help us should never have allowed it. She is not unlike the thousands of people who do not understand the evils which are part of the world God created. Why are innocent people hurt? Why are some people so blessed with health and wealth, and others, through no fault of their own, die homeless infected with disease. And if our close

CONTACT

ones do have to die, why can't we talk to them again. Why don't they communicate with us? We simply do not understand.

Once the misunderstanding is present, it is a short journey to statements which call into question exactly what God's nature is. We may conclude that there must be many gods in the world, as did the Athenians in Paul's time, or we may conclude that God is the figment of our imagination, as Ellie Arroway came to believe as a scientist.

We are believers, but it is very important for us to see exactly what we believe. We do not claim to know everything about God simply because we believe, nor can we explain well the problem of evil on a personal and global level. But, because of what we see around us, we are led to say that God really does exist, and at the same time, we know that we who occupy this world possess free wills. God therefore must have created us that way. Because of misuse of freedom, we can understand the evils in our world. But it still does not explain the ins and outs of why God works the way God does. In fact, maybe it is better for us not to understand, because then, perhaps, we will continue to search and "grope for him" as Paul writes. It is sad when intelligent people cease the searching because they think they have found a simple answer, because the answer will never be simple.

Preliminary Thought

1. What is the best human image of God that you can think of?
2. [The instructor may want to prepare for this question.] In this all-good world which God created, why do bad things happen to good people?
3. The meditation says that perhaps it is better for us not to understand God, because then, perhaps, we will continue to search and "grope for him." Do you agree and why or why not?
4. If you had a friend who did not believe in God, and you wanted to convince him/her that there was, how would you go about it?

Notes

CONTACT

Reflections/Ideas/Discussion

WHAT SCENE DURING THIS SESSION STRIKES YOU THE MOST AND WHY?

5. Scene analysis: The opening of the movie. What do you think Director Robert Zemeckis is "saying" by having the mind travel through the solar systems into the eye of the young Ellie Arroway?
6. Dialogue analysis: In answer to the question of whether there is life on other planets, the answer given is: "If it's just us, it seems like an awful waste of space." What do you think of the answer?
7. Analysis: Do you think it is a waste of time to study whether there is extra-terrestrial life? Yes or no and why?
8. Dialogue analysis: Palmer says that he is against the people who deify technology. Do you think that most scientists do that?
9. Dialogue analysis: Palmer says that he couldn't live with celibacy as a priest. Do you think that priests should have the option to marry? Yes or no and why?
10. Scene analysis: Palmer and Ellie are in bed together. There is obviously no desire for any commitment on the part of either one. Do such scenes of "casual sex" have any affect on young people? Yes or no and why?
11. Dialogue/scene analysis: Ellie obviously has "turned off" God because she didn't sense her questions to be answered and because her Dad died young. [Perhaps there is nothing more heart-rending than to watch nine-year-old Ellie trying to get her Dad to answer her CQ.] What, if anything, could have been said to Ellie to make her understand God's way?
12. Scene analysis: Ellie begs for money. Recalling Ellie's arguments that inventions like the airplane would never have been discovered if people hadn't worked in research, do you think that large amounts of money should be spent on a project like Ellie was interested in? Yes or no and why?
13. Dialogue analysis: Ellie is told to face reality and stop the project, but she is still determined. What are the principal elements of "being determined"?
14. Dialogue analysis: Palmer says on Larry King's program that the question he is asking in his book "Losing Faith" is: Are we happier as a human race, or are we better as a human race because of science and technology? Answer his question: Are we? Yes or no and why?

CONTACT

Notes

SESSION II

From: As Ellie is listening on the hood of her car, begins to hear a noise, and opens her eyes.

To: After Ellie and the religious fanatic (with long blond hair) stare at each other during Ellie's entrance into the reception.

Approximate time: 37 minutes.

Theme: Communication with each other is the single most important preparation for understanding each other.

Scripture: **James 3:2b-5** Communication through words can bring about great possibilities.

Doctrine/Application
[*Catechism of the Catholic Church* **reference:** numbers 2465-2470]

How important is communication in life? How important is communication between members of the same family? Indeed, how important is communication between people of different planets? As Ellie Arroway and her scientist friends discover that there is intelligent life on at least one other planet, suddenly communication becomes a primary concern. What do you say to them? What do you think they are saying to us? Whatever the answers, there is little doubt that the beginning of any relationship will be good or bad depending on the quality of communication.

The early Christians knew the importance of words and communication. The Christian letter of James is among the most practical of all the letters that are in the canon of the Bible, and a prominent place is given to the power of the tongue. "The tongue is a small member and yet has great pretensions" (James 3:5), the author of the letter of James says. Or in other words, even though the tongue may be small, great things can be accomplished because of the tongue's power to form words, and thus

CONTACT

communicate. The power of communication is a power than can bring planets, continents, cities and people together. Indeed, much good can be accomplished when we communicate well.

But unfortunately, evil comes into play also. Immediately after this passage in the letter of James, the author goes on to account how a "world of malice" can come about because of the tongue. Our concern with communication is not going to be as important as how to communicate with an alien planet, nor probably with any monumental accomplishment, but it will have everything to do with day to day living and the good and evil which communication can bring about. People who refuse to communicate with each other, whether in a family or in a community, often cause disruption and confusion and even hatred. Everyone of us has the opportunity to communicate well if we want; and when we do, we will begin to understand well.

Preliminary Thought

15. On a scale of 1-10 where 10 is high, how important would you rate "communication with others"? Why did you assign the number you did?
16. In your opinion, what are the characteristics of a person who has learned to communicate well?
17. Since it is reported that "lack of communication" is the number one cause of marriage breakdown, in what areas of communication do married couples have the most problems?
18. Do you believe that most young people communicate "well" with each other? Yes or no and why?

Notes

CONTACT

Reflection/Ideas/Discussion

WHAT SCENE DURING THIS SESSION STRIKES YOU THE MOST AND WHY?

19. Scene analysis: The scientists decide to tell everyone about the contact. If you woke up one morning to this on the news, what would be your first thought?
20. Scene analysis: Dr. Drumlin talks to the media as if it is his discovery. Do you think that people really are as proud and selfish as Drumlin is depicted here? Yes or no and why?
21. Analysis: As you saw for the first time that the image coming from the signal was Adolf Hitler, what was your first thought? Why did you feel the way you did?
22. Scene analysis: The military recommends that they take over the investigation. What are the advantages and disadvantages of such an action?
23. Scene analysis: The different types of people who come to New Mexico to get closer to the phenomenon. What do you think this scene says about America?
24. Scene analysis: Dr. Hadden and Ellie. Do you believe that there are people as smart as Dr. Hadden in the world? Yes or no and why?
25. Scene analysis: Why do many consider the contact to be hostile?
26. Scene analysis: The demonstrators at the reception. a) Do demonstrations such as this accomplish anything? b) In particular, do you believe that most religious demonstrations show "hatred" as this one does?

Notes

CONTACT

SESSION III

From: After Ellie and the religious fanatic (with long blond hair) stare at each other during Ellie's entrance into the reception.
To: After Ellie goes to the machine and looks at the spheres circling below her.
Approximate time: 35 minutes.

Theme: Religious fanaticism is not the same as religion.

Scripture: **Luke 22:47-53** Jesus shows his disciples what is really important in religion.

Doctrine/Application
[*Catechism of the Catholic Church* **reference:** numbers 109-119]

Biblical fundamentalism is the belief of individuals that a particular translation of the Bible is absolutely correct. Such believers will not accept any interpretation of the Bible given by the Church or Scripture scholars. For them, Scripture's and Jesus' words are to be taken literally, according to their own understanding of the translation of the Bible passage. It is wrong because it denies the truth of official interpretation and especially biblical scholarship.

It is wrong also because it can easily lead to fanaticism and misguided zeal. Witness the conduct of some religious leaders in the movie "Contact." In a religious fundamentalist's mind, there is little regard for scientific discovery, let alone the possibility of life on another planet. When scientist Ellie Arroway and her staff proclaim scientifically that they have proof of life on another planet, the biblical fundamentalist turned fanatic cannot allow such blasphemy.

Religious fanaticism is not the same as religion. Jesus admonishes his followers that a sword has no place in his kingdom, even though Jesus was about to suffer death. We know that some of his disciples were of the religious group called Zealots who desired the armed overthrow of the government. Jesus tells his disciple to put away his sword (Luke 22:51), in effect saying that armed defense is not an option for his kingdom, and more or less, it must be considered a fanatic approach to Jesus' doctrine.

Our Christian world is plagued with believers whose Christian belief comes very close to religious fanaticism. We may not see much evidence of an organized attack on scientific projects but there are indications that fanaticism has made inroads into religion. A Christian person bombs an abortion clinic because he believes abortion is wrong. A Bible-quoting lobbyist in a political party organizes the ruin of the reputation of a candidate for public office. A religion teacher in a Christian school teaches her students that high school age kissing is always a moral offense. All are examples of religious fanaticism. The answer to any fanaticism, religious included, is found only in knowledge, knowledge gained from the official interpretation of the Church and study of the Bible that comes from scholars dedicated to the truth.

Preliminary Thought

27. [The instructor may want to prepare for this question ahead of time. See *Catechism* reference for the *Doctrine/Application* above.] **Discuss biblical fundamentalism, giving some examples of erroneous beliefs.**
28. **The meditation interprets Jesus' action in the Garden as a statement that "armed defense is not an option in his kingdom." Do you think self-defense is part of the Christian belief? Yes or no and why? Discuss your answer in light of Jesus' action.**
29. **Discuss any examples that you have seen of religious fanaticism.**

Notes

Reflection/Ideas/Discussion

WHAT SCENE DURING THIS SESSION STRIKES YOU THE MOST AND WHY?

30. Dialogue analysis: Ellie talks to Palmer concerning God. a) She asks the question, "What if science simply reveals that God didn't exist in the first place?" What is your reply? b) What is your answer to the accusation from many atheists that "we have created God?" c) Can someone actually prove that there is love present? Yes or no and why?

CONTACT

31. Scene analysis: The "machine" will cost one/third of a trillion dollars. What is your opinion concerning the amount of time and money the United States spends on space exploration?
32. Dialogue analysis: Ellie tells Palmer that "for as long as I can remember, I've been searching for the reason why we're here." What is your answer as to why we are here.
33. Dialogue/scene analysis: Palmer interrogates Ellie in front of the committee, and asks the question which is key to the investigation: "Do you believe in God?" Ellie answers that she did not understand the relevance of the question. Do you believe that it is a fair question in these circumstances?
34. Scene analysis: Ellie goes to the testing of the machine. As a professional, she must rise above her personal feelings. Do you think that in our political society, the professionals "rise above" their personal feelings? Yes or no and why?
35. Scene analysis: The fanatic destroys himself, the people around him and the machine. Terrorists are among the most feared individuals in our world because of their dedication to a cause, since they will do anything, including suffering death, not unlike the kamikaze pilots of Japan. How should we of the free world deal with terrorists?
36. Scene analysis: Ellie is given the suicide pill. What do you think of the practice of giving "suicide" pills to people who are freely accepting severe danger?

Notes

CONTACT

SESSION IV

From: After Ellie goes to the machine and looks at the spheres circling below her.
To: End.
Approximate time: 35 minutes.

Theme: God is with us, no matter how we think.

Scripture: **Psalm 139:1-18** God is all-knowing and ever present.

Doctrine/Application
[*Catechism of the Catholic Church* reference: numbers 31-38]

The philosophy of a believer in God is an easy one. It may move into complicated theories and explanatory reasoning, but the foundation of faith is straight to the point: believers do not know whether what they believe is true. There may be every reason to believe in God. Psalm 139 has outlined such reasons very well. "Where can I go from your spirit, from your presence where can I flee? If I go up to the heavens, you are there; if I sink to the nether world, you are present there." (Psalm 139: 7-8) As the Psalmist points out, there may be indications that we indeed *should* believe in God, but in the final analysis, belief by its very nature cannot be certain.

Consequently, many scientists do not have an easy time with faith. It is especially true for scientists who have experienced difficult times and have reasoned themselves away from the belief in the existence of God. Ellie Arroway was such a scientist. If she had discovered anything about a Supreme Being, it was that there was no scientific proof for such an existence, and that fit her life just fine. She made that point eminently clear in her interview with the committee for the selection of a candidate to travel in the machine.

Then something happened. She won't be able to explain it. In fact, the people who interrogate her will turn away in disgust as she tries to explain her experience: "I had an experience," Ellie says, "I can't prove it. ... I was given something wonderful, ... a vision that tells us that we belong to something that is greater than ourselves, that we are not ... alone." Because of the vision, the scientist became a believer. As she tried to make sense of what happened to her, the very thing that she could never accept—faith in a Supreme Being—became a reality to her.

Not unlike scientists that want certitude before they will accept something, believers in a Supreme Being often find themselves wanting reasons to believe. They look for evidence, they explore possibilities. They create "belief scenarios." There is nothing wrong with such behavior for the believer. It becomes a problem when the believer creates a premise which demands a certitude which faith, by definition, can never give.

CONTACT

> ### Preliminary Thought
>
> 37. In your opinion, what is the best "proof" that God exists?
> 38. People experience God in many different ways in their lives. Discuss some experience that you have had where you felt God's presence.
> 39. According to research, most North American people believe in God. Do you think that most people "act" like they believe in God. Yes or no and why?

Notes

> ### Reflection/Ideas/Discussion
>
> **WHAT SCENE DURING THIS SESSION STRIKES YOU THE MOST AND WHY?**
>
> 40. Dialogue analysis: Ellie keeps saying "I'm okay to go." What is the driving force which moves a person to be an astronaut or to explore space?
> 41. Scene analysis: When she releases herself from her seat, the vibration ceases. The vibration was caused by the scientists' "addition" to the specifications of the machine. What are the conditions of our trust in another?
> 42. Dialogue analysis: As Ellie views the sight in front of her, she says that she wishes she were a poet to describe it. What is the most beautiful sight you have ever seen?
> 43. Dialogue analysis: Ellie's Dad's words—"You are an interesting species, an interesting mix. You're capable of such beautiful dreams and such horrible nightmares. You feel so lost, so cut off, so alone, only you're not. See, in all our searching, the only thing we've found that makes the emptiness bearable is each other." What strikes you the most about the quote? Why?

CONTACT

44. Dialogue analysis: Ellie's Dad tells Ellie that she has to make "small moves." What do you think he means?
45. Scene analysis: Ellie at the Senate hearing. a) Kitz implies that the whole adventure was made up by Hadden, the person that helped Ellie in the first place. Was there any way that Ellie could have convinced Kitz? Yes or no and why? b) Ellie's complete statement, a portion of which was quoted in the meditation: "I had an experience. I can't prove it. I can't even explain it, but everything that I know as a human being tells me that it was real. I was given something wonderful, something that changed me forever, a vision of the universe that tells us undeniably how tiny and insignificant and how rare and precious we all are; a vision that tells us that we belong to something that is greater than ourselves, that we are not, that none of us are, alone. I want to share that. I wish that everyone if even for one moment could feel that awe and humility and hope. That continues to be my wish." What is most striking about this statement and why?
46. Dialogue analysis: Palmer's statement concerning whether he believed Ellie: "As a person of faith, I'm bound by a different covenant than Dr. Arroway, but our goal is one and the same: the pursuit of truth. I believe her." What do you consider the primary truth?
47. Analysis: Having seen the movie "Contact," what message do you believe director Robert Zemeckis and author Carl Sagan (who wrote the novel on which the movie was based) are trying to convey?

Further Material

COURAGE UNDER FIRE

[This movie is rated "R" by the motion picture industry because of language.]

GENERAL THEME

The greatest thing that we can offer ourselves or others is the truth.

SESSION I
From: Begins right away.
To: During the flashback, after Captain Walden sees that she is hurt, and the movie returns to the present.
Approximate time: 38 minutes.

Theme: Sometimes our decisions cause consequences that affect us deeply.

Scripture: **Matthew 20:17-19** Jesus decides to travel to Jerusalem.

Doctrine/Application
[*Catechism of the Catholic Church* reference: numbers 1776-1802]

Decisions. Everybody makes them. Sometimes they have a major impact on our lives; sometimes, none. Sometimes, living with their consequences is easy. Sometimes, on the other hand, living with them can be among the most difficult things that we are ever called to do. Jesus made such a decision in his life. Colonel Nate Serling and Captain Karen Walden also made them in their lives.

In Matthew's Gospel, Jesus freely chooses to go to Jerusalem. It is a decision that will eventually lead to his death. Although not aware of the exact details, Jesus must have known that if the Scribes and Pharisees ever had a chance to take him into custody, they would do it. And Jerusalem was an easy place to do it. Nonetheless, he made the decision and as he had foreseen, suffered the consequences. (Matthew 20:17-19)

In the movie "Courage Under Fire," both Colonel Serling and Captain Walden had to make decisions on the same night in separate arenas of the same war. Both had consequences that were life-altering. But they understood what had to be done and they were willing to live with the consequences, as incredibly difficult as they were.

Young and old alike would do well to consider the consequences of decisions that they make. There are times when decisions may have such dire consequences that lives will literally never be the same. In fact, sometimes the consequences of the decisions will make it next to impossible to function in a normal way. Consequently, everyone

COURAGE UNDER FIRE

of us should try to measure all the ramifications of any decision that we make. We also are called in the final analysis to accept responsibility for decisions that we have made.

> ### Preliminary Thought
>
> 1. a) In general, what are the most important decisions we make in our lives? b) Go through each one and describe the principal consequences of the decision.
> 2. The movie takes place during the Persian Gulf War. a) What are the circumstances necessary in your opinion, for a "just" war? b) Do you believe that all of the wars in which your country has been involved are "just"? Discuss your answer.
> 3. Do you believe that most young people between the ages of 16 and 22 "think carefully" about decisions that they make? Yes or no and why?

Notes

> ### Reflection/Ideas/Discussion
>
> **WHAT SCENE DURING THIS SESSION STRIKES YOU THE MOST AND WHY?**
> 4. Scene analysis: Colonel Serling says a prayer before battle. Do you find this at all contradictory behavior? Yes or no and why?
> 5. Scene analysis: The killing that takes place. a) Do you believe that the killing that is shown in movies is too graphic for most viewers? Yes or no and why?
> b) Do you feel that our society is more violent because of such scenes in movies? Yes or no and why?

COURAGE UNDER FIRE

6. Dialogue analysis: Serling says to his subordinate: "I gave the order to fire." He admitted immediately that the fault was his. In general, do we Americans admit fault immediately? Yes or no and why?
7. Scene analysis: The military discovers the accident quickly. Did the military behave the way they should have in this case? Yes or no and why?
8. Scene analysis: Serling begins the letter to Mr. and Mrs. Boylar. Do you believe he should have immediately admitted to them what happened? Yes or no and why?
9. Scene analysis: Flashback as described by the originally downed helicopter crew. The crew admitted that they talked of surrendering. What is your personal feeling about surrendering to the enemy in time of war?
10. Scene analysis: Serling discovers for the first time that Walden is a woman. a) Obviously, the fact that she is a woman should make no difference at all. But, why does it make a difference? b) Discuss the advisability of women officers in the military, especially in combat situations.
11. Scene analysis: Serling drinking alcohol. Throughout the movie, it becomes obvious that Colonel Serling relied on alcohol to deaden the internal pain he was experiencing. It is a common enough way of approaching such pain. a) If you were a close friend of his, was there anything you could have done for him? Yes or no and why? b) Granted the internal pain being what it is, what *should* he have done?
12. Dialogue/scene analysis: Serling's wife tells him "I don't know what's happening here." Serling does not communicate with his wife about the things that are going on in his life and in his mind. a) What is the principal reason why many married people cannot communicate? b) Do you believe a general rule such as "we will always communicate with each other no matter what" is a good general rule for a married couple? Yes or no and why?
13. Dialogue analysis: Rody's wife comments that a woman wanting to be an officer was not a good thing. Do you think that there is any real difference between a woman wanting to be an officer and a man wanting the same thing? Yes or no and why?
14. Dialogue analysis: The language during the incident. Do you believe that there is really as much profanity in a military situation as displayed in the movie? Yes or no and why?

COURAGE UNDER FIRE

> **15. Scene analysis: Ilario is chain-smoking.** a) Aside from the medical problems connected with the action, in general, does "chain-smoking" indicate that there is something the matter with the person? Yes or no and why? b) Young people are smoking more and more in our society. Do you believe that the action of smoking could be describing a serious problem with young people? Yes or no and why?

Notes

SESSION II

From: During the flashback, after Captain Walden sees that she is hurt, and the movie returns to the present.

To: After Gardner says to Serling: "Eat something; you look awful" and walks away.

Approximate time: 37 minutes.

Theme: When we know the truth, we can never really hide it.

Scripture: **2 Corinthians 5:6-10** Paul reminds the Corinthians that their actions will be rewarded or punished.

Doctrine/Application
[*Catechism of the Catholic Church* reference: numbers 2464-2470]

Paul the apostle was interested in getting his Corinthian converts to understand that one day the truth about how they were behaving would come to light. "We must all appear before the judgment seat of Christ," Paul writes, "so that each one may receive recompense, according to what he did in the body, whether good or evil." (2 Corinthians 5:10) Paul knew that their behavior was involved in covering up the truth, something he knew would not happen in the next life, even if it could happen in this one.

COURAGE UNDER FIRE

In the movie "Courage Under Fire," Colonel Serling knew that the truth that was punishing his conscience had to come to light. The Boylar family deserved to know the truth. At the same time, he wanted to know the truth about what really happened with Captain Walden. He reasoned that obviously someone was lying, perhaps hiding something, and that if he worked on the case hard enough, the truth would surface. In both his case and the Walden case, he knew that the truth could not be hidden for too long.

There are many instances in our lives when we may be trying to hide the truth. As we search our consciences, we may find that we are doing something that is wrong. It may be that our lives are headed the wrong direction because we have made decisions that have moved us down a path which is dangerous. It may be that we are using other people for our own desires. Perhaps we are involved too much in relationships which are controlling us.

Hiding the truth is often dangerous to our psychological and physical health. Even in this life, it might even be impossible since some day the truth will surface in one way or another.

Preliminary Thought

16. Do you agree with the theme of this session, namely: "When we know the truth, we can never really hide it"? Yes or no and why?
17. As you consider "facing the truth" in your life, what are the principal ways to go about it?
18. Many young people make decisions early in their lives that lead them to the wrong decisions. What can be done to show them what they are really doing?

Notes

COURAGE UNDER FIRE

Reflection/Ideas/Discussion

WHAT SCENE DURING THIS SESSION STRIKES YOU THE MOST AND WHY?

19. Dialogue analysis: Ilario speaks of the young children doing actions and never thinking about the consequences. In general, do you believe that young people in high school and college think about the consequences of their actions? Yes or no and why?

20. Ilario lies to Serling about sending the letter to Walden's parents. Obviously, this will easily be confirmed to be a lie—which does happened during this session. Why do people lie even though they feel fairly certain that the truth will come out anyway?

21. Scene analysis: Karen Walden was divorced, raising her child alone. a) Do you believe that a full-time army career could easily lead to divorce? Yes or no and why? b) What principal elements should be present for a single mother to raise her child well?

22. Dialogue analysis: Serling's wife mentions that the family is all losing their lives. When a father is absent from the family, either psychologically or physically, what areas of family living are affected most?

23. Dialogue analysis: Serling tells his commanding officer that "someone has to be accountable" for things that should be explained. Do you believe that in general, we understand the necessity for accountability, especially when we are the ones who must be accountable for actions? Yes or no and why?

24. Dialogue/scene analysis: Monfriez's description of Walden's behavior was totally different from what Ilario said, and according to Monfriez, she was a coward and full of fear. a) Do you believe that there are soldiers who are *not* afraid in combat? Yes or no and why? b) Following along the same thought, do you believe the movie versions of people like Rambo and others who show absolutely no fear as they are fighting the enemy? Yes or no and why?

25. Dialogue analysis: Serling calls his wife, telling her that he has a pint and didn't want to drink it. Should his wife have behaved differently than she did? Yes or no and why?

26. Dialogue/scene analysis: Serling and his commanding officer on the golf course. Serling accepts the possibility of a "dishonorable discharge" rather than submit an incomplete report or one that is false. Do you believe that *most* officers would behave the way Serling did? Yes or no and why?

COURAGE UNDER FIRE

> **27. Scene analysis:** Serling agrees to allow Gardner to have the tape of communications on the night that Boylar's tank was destroyed. Given the fact that it was confidential material, in your opinion, should he have done it? Yes or no and why?

Notes

SESSION III

From: After Gardner says to Serling: "Eat something; you look awful" and walks away.

To: End.

Approximate time: 37 minutes.

Theme: The truth will always set us free.

Scripture: **John 8:31-38** Jesus speaks of the importance of truth.

Doctrine/Application
[*Catechism of the Catholic Church* **reference:** numbers 2475-2487]

In the third session of "Courage Under Fire," Colonel Nate Serling clearly states what should be a guide for every Christian in the world. He tells his commanding officer that the military must tell the complete truth and until they do, they dishonor every soldier that ever died in combat. It is the statement that implies a Christian understanding of life since it was Jesus who supplied the reasoning for it. He told his disciples: "The truth will set you free." (John 8:32)

Every family in our world perhaps stresses at one time or another time the importance of telling the truth to each other. Parents teach their children over and over the evils of lying and what it does to them. But all too often, the common complaint of

COURAGE UNDER FIRE

the parents of children and teenagers is that their children do not tell the truth or do not tell the complete truth. In fact, it happens so often that a concerned person might well wonder whether young people even understand the importance of the truth.

There is no doubt that the truth will set us free as Jesus instructs his disciples. The question must be asked however whether we, and especially our young, truly accept that fact or not. If Christian people do not truly understand the importance of the truth as a fundamental step in living a good Christian life, perhaps there will be no truth sacred enough to honor.

Preliminary Thought

28. Do you believe that the military in particular makes a habit of "telling the complete truth"? Yes or no and why?
29. Jesus makes a point that his followers should tell the truth. Do you think that the only reason why we should tell the truth is because it is a belief of our religion? Yes or no and why?
30. Do you believe that in general, young people really understand the importance of telling the truth? Yes or no and why?

Notes

Reflection/Ideas/Discussion

WHAT SCENE DURING THIS SESSION STRIKES YOU THE MOST AND WHY?

COURAGE UNDER FIRE

31. Scene analysis: Steve Altmeyer refuses to talk to Serling by making the medicine put him to sleep. Obviously, this is yet another way of blocking the truth when it hurts. As you consider how people block the truth, what are the most common ways that young people in particular block it?
32. Scene analysis: Monfriez pulls the weapon and directs it at Serling, accusing Serling of killing his own men. Serling admits it without hesitation. When the truth is difficult to admit, in general, *why* do we not want to admit it?
33. Dialogue analysis: Serling calls Monfriez a good soldier, and he probably was. Why is it that someone who is good at some vocation will often have difficulties in the same field also? Discuss your answer.
34. Scene analysis: Monfriez commits suicide, the ultimate block to the truth. In general, why do young people in particular commit suicide?
35. Dialogue analysis: Ilario admits using drugs, another block to the truth. a) In general, why do young people begin to use drugs in high school or college? b) Do you believe that programs such as the DARE program for elementary children is helpful in preventing the use of drugs? Yes or no and why?
36. Scene analysis: Ilario's flashback. a) Captain Walden cries (also in Monfriez's flashback) and calls it "tension." Do you agree with her analysis? Yes or no and why? b) Captain Walden is obviously strong in her dealing with Monfriez. Do you think that she should have behaved any differently? Yes or no and why? c) The soldiers all lie about Captain Walden, telling the rescue helicopter pilot that she was dead. It is a statement comparable to murder. Is there any way at all that their action could have been justified? Yes or no and why? d) In general, is murder always wrong? Yes or no and why?
37. Character analysis: Ilario. In particular, what do you think is Ilario's future?
38. Scene analysis: In a sense, the General explains away what the military did. In your opinion, do you think this is a "common practice" for United States military? Yes or no and why?
39. Scene analysis: Risking discharge from the army (one would guess) Serling visits the Boylar's and asks forgiveness. Do you believe that in the same situation most parents would grant forgiveness as readily as the Boylar's? Yes or no and why?
40. Scene analysis: Serling salutes at Walden's grave after he places his medal on the grave. It is a sign of total respect and honor. Who is a person that you respect the most right now and why?

COURAGE UNDER FIRE

> **41. If there is one thing the movie "Courage Under Fire" should teach the military establishment of your country, what would it be?**

Further Material

DEAD MAN WALKING

[This movie has been rated "R" by the motion picture industry because of violence.]

GENERAL THEME

There can be true conversion only when a person begins to accept responsibility.

SESSION I
From: Begins right away.
To: As Sr. Helen is talking to Earl Delacroix who says "tears me up."
Approximate time: 38 minutes.

Theme: Helping someone else involves more than simply talking about it.

Scripture: **1 John 4:11-16**   The love of one for the other.

Doctrine/Application
[*Catechism of the Catholic Church* **reference:** numbers 1889, 2196]

The first letter of John is probably the best statement on the importance of love that we have in the Christian Scriptures. The argument of the author is really very simple: "God is love, and whoever remains in love remains in God and God in him." (1 John 4:16) The goal of every Christian must be to remain in God. Since the definition of God is love, then it only stands to reason that the person who desires God must love. Love means not only love of God, but also the expression of the love of God, namely, love of this earth as well. Primary among the things of creation are the men and women who make up our world. "This is how we know that we remain in him and he in us," the author writes. (1 John 4:13) Consequently, the Christian *must* love one another if they seek the love of God.

Sr. Helen Prejean, C.S.J. believed the doctrine of love. She had been taught it early on in life by her parents, and it was a significant part of her training for religious life. Interpreting the love of neighbor to include especially the poor of the world, she had asked her superiors to give her the opportunity to work with the poor. She thought she "loved" people as she worked with the people who really needed her help. But her understanding of love was to grow even more, when she decided to write to a person on death row. The letter was to force her to see love on a much deeper level.

Christians claim to love others. We have been taught that we must do it since we began to listen to our parents who also had been taught to love. However, many times our love has remained only on the surface: we give lip service to love. We express our

DEAD MAN WALKING

love by giving to people who will appreciate us, for example; we love, but without any real cost to our comfortable lives. The test of love comes when care for others goes beyond our comfort level and begins to cause pain. Love of others may not require heroic stands or martyrdom, but if it does, the true Christian will carry it out.

Preliminary Thought

1. a) Do you believe that most people in our society really love God today? Yes or no and why? b) Do you believe that most people in our society really show a love of neighbor? Yes or no and why?
2. a) Do you think that religious orders of women are important to our society? Yes or no and why? b) Why are young women not choosing the vocation of religious life today?
3. Explain the meditation's statement: "We love, but without any real cost to our comfortable lives."

Notes

Reflections/Ideas/Discussion

WHAT SCENE DURING THIS SESSION STRIKES YOU THE MOST AND WHY?

4. Scene analysis: Director Tim Robbins chooses to "tell the story" of the killings by interspersing scenes of the murders throughout the movie. The scenes of the murders are the reason that the movie is rated "R." a) Do you think that the scenes so far are depicted too violently? Yes or no and why?

b) In general, do violent movies "influence" the young mind in a strong way? Yes or no and why? c) Violence has been depicted more graphically through the years. In general, do you think there is too much violence depicted in movies and television? Yes or no and why?

5. Dialogue analysis: Matthew remarks to Sr. Helen that she "comes from money." Do you think that people who have a "background of money" can ever understand what it means to be poor? Yes or no and why?

6. Dialogue analysis: Matthew says that there is no one with money on death row. What do you think he means and explain why you think he is correct or not.

7. Dialogue analysis: Matthew tells Sr. Helen that he didn't kill anyone. a) In general, can you really believe someone on death row? Yes or no and why? b) What would you suggest as characteristics that must be present in a person in order to trust that the person is telling the truth?

8. Scene analysis: (in the flashback) Sr. Helen remembers that she and her playmates killed an animal. In your opinion, what is the meaning of the scene?

9. Scene analysis: Sr. Helen is stopped by a highway patrolmen and is allowed to go with a warning simply because she is a religious sister. Do you agree with the patrolman's decision? Yes or no and why?

10. Character analysis: Matthew Poncelet. From what you have seen so far, how would you describe Matthew Poncelet?

11. Dialogue/scene analysis: Sr. Helen visits Mrs. Poncelet. a) Do you believe Matthew's upbringing had anything to do with the way he turned out? b) Mrs. Poncelet asks the question of where she went wrong. Did she do anything wrong? Yes or no and why?

12. Dialogue/scene analysis: Sr. Helen's family reminds her that because her heart is "large," others may take advantage of her. If one allows another to take advantage of him/her, is it necessarily a bad thing? Yes or no and why?

13. Dialogue/scene analysis: Matthew asks Sr. Helen about what she gave up to be a religious sister. Specifically, do you believe that perpetual celibacy is a value that should be pursued in our society? Yes or no and why?

14. Dialogue analysis: Matthew says that he is a person who deserves respect. True or false and why?

15. Dialogue/scene analysis: Hilton Barker explains that we have taken the "horror" out of the death penalty. True or false and why?

DEAD MAN WALKING

> 16. Dialogue/scene analysis: Mr. Delacroix talks to Sr. Helen. a) It is true that Sr. Helen did not contact his family or the Percy's. In your opinion, should she have contacted them? Yes or no and why? b) What are some "general rules" that people should follow when they perform an act of charity?
> 17. Scene analysis: Sr. Helen visits Earl Delacroix. What is most striking about this scene so far in your opinion? Why?

Notes

SESSION II
From: As Sr. Helen is talking to Earl Delacroix who says "tears me up."
To: After Sr. Helen's mother says, "A mother's arms are strong when her child's in danger," and she takes Sr. Helen's hand.
Approximate time: 39 minutes.

Theme: Often decisions that follow from correct convictions are controversial, and the one who makes them will lose friends.

Scripture: **Acts 15:36-41** Paul and Barnabas separate over a disagreement.

Doctrine/Application
[*Catechism of the Catholic Church* reference: numbers 1776-1794]
Since Paul and Barnabas had worked closely together from early on in the ministry of spreading the cause of Jesus Christ, one could safely assume that they were friends. But it is a fact of human nature that friendship does not easily change people with strong personalities. As a result, because of the personal convictions that people with strong personalities have, friendships may lessen somewhat. One is led to believe that such was the case between Paul and Barnabas. Both were strong, both were right in a

DEAD MAN WALKING

sense. So, perhaps the only outcome of their disagreement could have been to separate and probably lessen their friendship. (Acts 15:36-41)

Sr. Helen did not change her strong personality and convictions when she took the veil of the Sisters of St. Joseph. If anything, her beliefs only strengthened with her religious training. She felt strongly about how religious sisters should dress, what their ministry should be, how wrong the death penalty was, and that all people should be able to die with dignity. It was almost inevitable then, that she would lose some friends in her life. During the first session and this session of the movie "Dead Man Walking," we can easily see exactly what her strong personal convictions do to those around her, especially those with equally strong convictions.

In many ways, a Christian must be counter-cultural. Studying the Scriptures, Christians should see that Jesus had very strong opinions, and as a result, lost many one-time followers. Consequently, the follower of Jesus may have opinions which are both strong and divisive. Simply put, there are many who will disagree with them. Perhaps one of the most difficult areas for a young person in today's world is the feeling of rejection which may come from friends because of strong Christian beliefs. In fact, the young person may experience so much strong rejection that they eventually give up some Christian beliefs that they have held since elementary school. Young Christians must be aware of both the moral truth they profess *and* the strength of the consequences of their beliefs.

What's more, belief means trust. There can only be trust within a real, live relationship. Therefore there must be a growing relationship with God in order for faith and moral truth to be real.

Preliminary Thought

18. As you study Paul and Barnabas' disagreement, in your opinion, is there any compromise that should have been reached? Yes or no and why?
19. As you study your life and the world around you, what issues do you consider most important?
20. What moral beliefs of elementary school do many young people give up when they get to high school and college?
21. [The instructor may want to prepare for this question ahead of time.] Much of the material of the movie "Dead Man Walking" deals with the death penalty. What is your opinion concerning the death penalty? Is it right or wrong? Why? [See *Catechism of the Catholic Church* numbers 2263-2267.]

DEAD MAN WALKING

Notes

Reflection/Ideas/Discussion

WHAT SCENE DURING THIS SESSION STRIKES YOU THE MOST AND WHY?

22. Dialogue analysis: Mr. Delacroix explains to Sr. Helen that when you lose someone, one is only left with memories. Explain how memories can be both good and bad.

23. Dialogue/scene analysis: The prison chaplain tells Sr. Helen that the only thing a spiritual advisor should do is get Matthew back to the Sacraments. Explain why this approach is incomplete.

24. Dialogue/scene analysis: Sr. Helen and Matthew's conversation. a) Sr. Helen asks Matthew whether he reads the Bible. Why is reading the Bible so important for the Christian? b) Why are the Christian Scriptures (New Testament) better to read than the Hebrew Scriptures (Old Testament)? c) They speak of racial prejudice. Define racial prejudice. d) Do you think that racial prejudice is still a "big problem" in North America among young people? Yes or no and why?

25. Scene analysis: The religious sisters "demonstrate" with prayer against the death penalty as the death penalty is enacted. Do you believe that this type of demonstration serves a good purpose? Yes or no and why?

26. Dialogue/scene analysis: Sr. Helen talks to Mr. and Mrs. Percy. a) They were civil to Sr. Helen only when they thought she agreed with them. As Christians, how do you think they should have behaved? b) What if anything do you think Sr. Helen could have done differently with the Percy's?

DEAD MAN WALKING

27. Scene analysis: Sr. Helen accompanies Mr. Delacroix to the support group. Why are such groups helpful to the participants?
28. Dialogue/scene analysis: Sr. Helen talks to a guard who helps prepare the convict for execution. Do you think that a Christian should take part in the killing of anyone? Yes or no and why?
29. Dialogue analysis: The chaplain tells Sr. Helen that the prison does not allow music for the condemned. Why do you think there is such a rule?
30. Scene analysis: Sr. Helen faints. No doubt, stress had something to do with her lightheadedness. Where do you think she felt the most stress?
31. Scene analysis: a) The prison officials did not tell Matthew what happened to Sr. Helen. Why do you think they did not tell him? b) Sr. Helen does not dwell on her ailments and listens only to Matthew. It is a mark of maturity to put all of one's attention to the other rather than try to explain one's own situation. Do you believe most young people spend too much time thinking of themselves? Yes or no and why?
32. Scene analysis: As Sr. Helen talks of the truth, Matthew begins to think about what he did. a) Do you believe that most people really *want* to own up to what they have done? Yes or no and why? b) In general, do young people accept responsibility for their actions? Yes or no and why?

Notes

SESSION III

From: After Sr. Helen's mother says, "A mother's arms are strong when her child's in danger," and she takes Sr. Helen's hand.
To: End.
Approximate time: 39 minutes.

Theme: Admitting the truth always enables one to live and die well.

DEAD MAN WALKING

Scripture: **John 8:31-36**   The truth will set a person free.

Doctrine/Application
[*Catechism of the Catholic Church* reference: numbers 2462-2470]

Matthew Poncelet found himself on a long journey in the movie "Dead Man Walking." He had never expected to take it; it had only come about after his decision to write a letter. Sr. Helen became his guide, leading him through small talk and saving-face conversation, gradually taking him to a point of acceptance of responsibility. But such acceptance was not easy. Thinking about his behavior for the first time in his life, he had finally come to the point of conversion. He finally was beginning to feel free.

Jesus testified to the feeling that psychologists have been writing about since Jesus' death. "The truth will set you free," Jesus said to those who believed in him. (John 8:32) The truth has always enabled humankind to live well. It brings about a spiritual basis for clear conscience and stability in a world where so much is changing, as well as a psychological sense of well-being. Leading people to feel good about themselves and what they believe and stand for, living the truth and admitting the truth is the way to a happy life, and even a happy death.

Young and old alike must discover this fact about the truth. Far too many people live a lie in one form or another. They choose a life of pleasure which is only hiding the pain of loneliness. Those who are rich display their riches to earn the respect that they will not give to others. Those who find themselves with power, even at the lowest level, often desire to use their power on others because of their own inadequacy. What we need in our world is Jesus' simple approach to the truth so that we can freely pursue our lives and feel good about it at the same time.

Preliminary Thought

33. **Do you think that most "hardened criminals" ever bring themselves to seriously consider why they have done? Yes or no and why?**
34. **The meditation mentions a clear conscience. What do you think makes up a clear conscience? [See *Catechism of the Catholic Church*, numbers 1783-1785.]**
35. **The meditation maintains that many people live a lie. In what ways do you find that young people in particular "live a lie"?**

DEAD MAN WALKING

Notes

Reflection/Ideas/Discussion

WHAT SCENE DURING THIS SESSION STRIKES YOU THE MOST AND WHY?

36. Dialogue analysis: The guard's statement to Sr. Helen that she should be teaching children. In the Catholic Church, religious sisters in general, are giving more time to other ministries rather than education. Do you believe this is good or bad for the Catholic Church? Why?

37. Dialogue analysis: The guard and Sr. Helen argue about the death penalty. When someone feels strongly about some particular issue, do you believe it is worthwhile to "argue" with them? Why or why not?

38. Scene analysis: Matthew visits his family for the last time. If you had only a couple hours with your family before your death, what topic would you consider the most important?

39. Scene analysis: As Director Tim Robbins flashes back to the death scene, do you believe that Walter and Hope were "inviting" problems by parking so far away for their love activity? Yes or no and why?

40. Dialogue analysis: Sr. Helen tells Matthew not to die in anger. As you look at human beings, do you think that many live and die in anger? Yes or no and why?

41. Dialogue analysis: Sr. Helen reminds Matthew that he is blaming others. Do you think that most people blame others when something wrong happens in their lives? Yes or no and why?

DEAD MAN WALKING

42. Scene analysis: Sr. Helen prays as she visits the restroom. a) As you consider "prayer," what are the times that people usually pray? What are the times when people *should* pray? b) Give your own definition of prayer. [See *Catechism of the Catholic Church* numbers 2607-2615.]
43. Dialogue analysis: Matthew finally admits his guilt to Sr. Helen, accepting "responsibility" for both of the young people's deaths. When admitting guilt, why is it so important to actually *say* the words?
44. Dialogue analysis: Sr. Helen calls Matthew a "son of God." What do you think was her meaning?
45. Dialogue analysis: Matthew says that he hopes his death gives Walter and Hope's parents some relief. Do you think it is possible that their parents really could receive any consolation from his death? Yes or no and why?
46. Dialogue analysis: Sr. Helen sings the song "Be Not Afraid." The instructor may want to obtain a copy of it and review it with the class.
47. Dialogue analysis: Matthew asks permission for Sr. Helen to touch him. Why do you think the act of touching was so important for Matthew?
48. Dialogue analysis: Matthew's closing words: (edited) "I don't want to leave this world with hate in my heart. I ask for your forgiveness. I hope my death gives you some relief. I think killing is wrong whether it's me, you'all, or your government." What is most impressive about the statement?
49. Scene analysis: Matthew dies. a) As we think of our own deaths, however they come, what important thought do you hope to keep in mind? b) Assuming that Director Tim Robbins is making a statement with the scene of Matthew's death, what is it?
50. Analysis: Earl Delacroix. As you have noted his actions and interactions with Sr. Helen during the show, do you think he will ever be able to forgive Matthew Poncelet? Yes or no and why?
51. In your opinion, what is the primary lesson of "Dead Man Walking"?

Notes

JURASSIC PARK

GENERAL THEME

People who work with unknown powers often end up hurting themselves and others.

SESSION I

From: Begins right away.
To: After Dr. Grant tries to ride in a different car from the children, and the voice from the loudspeaker says, "Everyone must be on the dock for the 1900 hours departure."
Approximate time: 40 minutes.

Theme: The results of our incredible technology must be regulated by the principles of God and not by the world.

Scripture: **Genesis 2:1-4** God creates the world.

Doctrine/Application
[*Catechism of the Catholic Church* reference: numbers 279-301]

Christians believe that God created the world. They have no doubt about it, and the Scriptures verify it, especially the first two chapters of the first book of the Bible, Genesis. There is much debate on *how* the world was created, and whether the words of Scripture should be taken literally, but there is no doubt of the religious truth. How ever the world was created, *God* did it. Further, God set aside the "seventh day" for rest. Looked at from the point of view of keeping holy the Sabbath, we can understand a day of rest, but perhaps there is another reason for the creation of the "seventh day." Perhaps God was saying to us that at least every week, we must remember the presence of God, always realizing that God is truly in charge of the world. Perhaps, also, God was telling us that if we try to live our world on our own power, we will end up hurting people.

The creators of the theme park called "Jurassic Park" in the movie of the same name were probably God-believing men and women. In their mind, there may indeed have been a higher power who was responsible for our world. But, when their minds were taken with the incredible technology that they possessed, and more importantly, with what the incredible technology could create, they lost sight of God's presence. As

JURASSIC PARK

Dr. Malcomb suggests in this session of "Jurassic Park," it is a dangerous time in people's lives when raw technology takes over life.

The intelligence of men and women can do incredible things. It is no longer science-fiction to produce a "Jurassic Park" in our world. In fact, we may be within a few years of conquering the complete knowledge of DNA (deoxyribonucleic acid) technology, and as a result, open possibilities of further unbelievable discoveries. We must learn to approach such times with respect for God, always remembering the power of God even as we continue to advance our technology.

Preliminary Thought

1. **According to statistics, most people believe that God created the world. Do you think that in general, our society shows that belief in action? Yes or no and why?**
2. **Do you believe that in our world where we see such incredible technology that we have a tendency to forget about God and think we are in control? Yes or no and why?**
3. **Do you think that we should keep advancing the technology of understanding DNA to the point of "cloning" people? Yes or no and why?**

Notes

Reflection/Ideas/Discussion

WHAT SCENE DURING THIS SESSION STRIKES YOU THE MOST AND WHY?

JURASSIC PARK

4. Scene analysis: The scientists collect data on dinosaurs. Do you believe that society should spend as much money as they do on things like archeological digs and scientific searches for lost artifacts? Yes or no and why?
5. Scene analysis: Dennis Nedry accepts the money to obtain the species from the island. Why is money such a determining factor in our world today?
6. Analysis: The amazing technology that created the movie "Jurassic Park". Do you think that it is a good thing to spend as much money on movies as is done today? Yes or no and why?
7. Dialogue analysis: "We're going to make a fortune with this place." Again, the stress is on money. Do you think it is true to say that money is the root of all evil? Yes or no and why?
8. Scene analysis: The owners of the park also breed velociraptors which are lethal at eight months. Why do you think they wanted to breed them at all?
9. Dialogue analysis: Ian Malcolm's and Alan Grant's speech (paraphrased): "Don't you see the inherent danger in what you are doing. Genetic power is the most awesome force there is. You have had no discipline as you attain it. You don't take any responsibility for it. You simply achieved it as fast as you could. Dinosaurs had their shot, and nature selected them for extinction. What you call discovery, I call the rape of the natural world. They will defend themselves violently if necessary. Dinosaurs and man have been subtly drawn together and we don't know what will happen." What part of the speech impresses you the most and why?
10. Scene analysis: Obviously Dr. Grant does not like children. If you could argue with Dr. Grant about the importance of children, what would be your main argument?

Notes

JURASSIC PARK

SESSION II

From: After Dr. Grant tries to ride in a different car from the children, and the voice from the loudspeaker says, "Everyone must be on the dock for the 1900 hours departure."

To: As the scientists are in the car with the dinosaur chasing them, and Malcolm says, "Think they'll have that on the tour?"

Approximate time: 41 minutes.

Theme: When our technology is not regulated by the principles of God, selfishness takes over.

Scripture: **Genesis 11:1-9**   Early men and women sin by wanting to be like God.

Doctrine/Application
[*Catechism of the Catholic Church* **reference:** numbers 2540]

The story of the Tower of Babel is an interesting one. In the story, all people are speaking the same language which leads them to want to build a skyscraper to reach heaven that they might have "a name for themselves," (Genesis 11:4) that is, to be like God. God subsequently, looks down from heaven and can barely make it out, even though the people think it is a tremendous monument, and so God must come down to see it. When he does, he recognizes their selfish desires, and decides to confuse their languages. The story shows that God is still in charge, even though human beings may selfishly think that they should be.

If the scientists of Jurassic Park had recognized God's importance, the theme park idea would probably have been abandoned. The dangers should have been obvious. Although they soon discovered that they were working with concepts that involved higher powers than they had, their selfishness pressed them on in their adventure. They were not about to abandon their discovery even if it did mean that people might be hurt. In place of God, selfishness had taken over their reasoning. In fact, every time that we allow our technology and creative desires to govern our lives without accepting the principles of God, our selfishness will take over.

We do not possess the technology that produced a "Jurassic Park," but we do have many modern conveniences that make our lives easier. We have access to things like the Internet and computer technology that becomes more proficient every day. Just as a Christian's life throughout the past was regulated by the principles of God, it should be even more so today. The principles of good living do not change just because we grow in technological awareness. We still must have profound respect for the things of this earth and for the people who make it up. A person skilled in technology who forgets

JURASSIC PARK

the principles of God is likely to choose in a selfish manner, as did the scientists of Jurassic Park.

Preliminary Thought

11. Define selfishness as you understand it.
12. The meditation refers to the "principles of God." In your opinion, what are the most important "principles of God" that people should follow?
13. Specifically as you think of computers, the Internet, e-mail, and computer technology, what do you think the "principles of God" would lay down as guidelines?

Notes

Reflections/Ideas/Discussion

WHAT SCENE DURING THIS SESSION STRIKES YOU THE MOST AND WHY?

14. Character analysis: Dennis Nedry, the computer expert. Obviously, he is a man who likes money, but he also seems prone to arguments. From what you have seen of him, what do you think his character is like?
15. Scene analysis: The visitors get out of the car, ignoring any danger. Why do young people especially seem to ignore danger (e.g., reckless driving, taking unnecessary chances, etc.)?
16. Scene analysis: Dr. Sattler goes into the dinosaur's "droppings". She is obviously dedicated to her work. In your opinion, do most people have this type of dedication to their work? Yes or no and why?

JURASSIC PARK

> 17. **Scene analysis:** Malcolm and Grant talk about marriage, with Malcolm's comment that he is married "occasionally." Do you think that most married people have this flippant an attitude toward marriage? Yes or no and why?
> 18. **Scene analysis:** The lawyer left the kids by themselves. Do you think most adults would behave this way? Yes or no and why?
> 19. **Scene analysis:** Grant distracts the large dinosaur with flares. Obviously, an act of heroism, since the dinosaur is looking for food. In your life right now, discuss any acts of "heroism" that you have seen.
> 20. **Scene analysis:** The raptor kills Dennis. There is almost a sense of "he deserves it" as one watches the scene. Is this a "Christian" feeling to have? Yes or no and why?
> 21. **Scene analysis:** Lex does not want Dr. Grant to leave her, since she remembers that the lawyer left. Younger people are affected by adult behavior, often in a profound way. Do you believe that most adults are aware of the example they are setting for young people? Yes or no and why?

Notes

SESSION III

From: As the scientists are in the car with the dinosaur chasing them, and Malcolm says, "Think they'll have that on the tour?"

To: End.

Approximate time: 39 minutes.

Theme: Even with the most advanced technology, people remain the most important creation.

Scripture: **Luke 24:25-27** Jesus suffered death and rose from the dead for our redemption.

JURASSIC PARK

Doctrine/Application
[*Catechism of the Catholic Church* **reference: numbers 571-573, 601]**

Even though their adventure was accomplished in an incredible way, the scientists of Jurassic Park finally discover that their fantasy could not be controlled. Eventually, they had to choose between people and their own creation. They choose people, but with a little reluctance, since they did not want all of their technology to be wasted. Their love of others may be a factor in their eventual departure from the incredible island, but one is led to believe that if there were a way, they would choose otherwise. Too often, we find ourselves flirting with evil rather than wanting to help human beings.

This never was the case with Jesus Christ. After his resurrection from the dead, Jesus realized completely what his role had been, as he explains to the disciples who were on their way to Emmaus. "Was it not necessary that the Messiah should suffer these things and enter into his glory?" (Luke 24:26) He explains to the disciples that from the beginning of the Hebrew era, the Messiah was interested in people, in their salvation, and he came to earth with that thought in mind, and no other. People were of the highest importance for God, even to the point of giving God's only Son.

The Christian must have the same love for fellow human beings. Even with all of our technology and computer wizardry, we can never forget that this earth is the beginning of life for people. Robots, computer-generated magic, and incredible accomplishments notwithstanding, *people* remain most important. The more we understand that, even in the face of technology, the more Christian we become. And the more we will comprehend that people must receive more respect than created machines.

Preliminary Thought

22. The meditation's statement: "Too often, we find ourselves flirting with evil rather than wanting to help human beings." True or false, and why?
23. Discuss the Christian doctrine of "redemption" and exactly what it should mean for us at the present time.
24. a) In what situations do you find "love of others" best portrayed? b) Where do you find it lacking the most?

JURASSIC PARK

Notes

Reflection/Ideas/Discussion

WHAT SCENE DURING THIS SESSION STRIKES YOU THE MOST AND WHY?

25. Scene analysis: Dr. Grant allows the kids to get closer to him. What do you think has changed in Dr. Grant to allow this closeness?
26. Dialogue analysis: Dr. Sattler tells John that she didn't have enough respect for the power. If she had the respect, what would she have done?
27. Scene analysis: The raptors try to get Dr. Sattler and the children. Was there anything that Dr. Sattler and the children could have done differently? Yes or no and why?
28. Scene analysis: Do you think that the terror and violence of the raptor scenes have any negative effect on young children? Yes or no and why?
29. Scene analysis: Dr. Sattler, Dr. Grant and the children are completely trapped by the raptors before the Tyrannosaurus attacks the raptors. There was no way out of the situation. What do you think they should have done?
30. What is the most important lesson of the movie "Jurassic Park"?

Further Material

ROMEO AND JULIET

GENERAL THEME

Love present between two young people in families that hate one another often leads to a tragic end.

SESSION I
[Corresponding to Shakespeare's Act I, Scene I to Act II, Scene II (middle)]
From: Begins right away.
To: After Romeo and Juliet fall into the water.
Approximate time: 38 minutes.

Theme: First love may be one of the strongest emotions young people ever feel.

Scripture: **Genesis 24:63-67** The love of Isaac and Rebekah.

Doctrine/Application
[*Catechism of the Catholic Church* reference: numbers 2337-2350]

Reading the story of Isaac and Rebekah in the Book of Genesis, one easily sees that God blessed the union from the very beginning. It also seems as though Rebekah and Isaac were in love from the very beginning. After Abraham's servant brought Rebekah, the one whom God had chosen, to Isaac, there must have been little doubt in Isaac's mind that this was his true love. It was so strong that the author of Genesis remarks, "In his love for her, Isaac found solace after the death of his mother." (Genesis 24:67) Since it was the first love for each of them, it probably was the strongest emotion connected with love either had ever felt.

The tragedy of "Romeo and Juliet" as written by William Shakespeare and also presented by director Baz Luhrmann, did not begin with tragedy. It began with love at first sight. Romeo of the house of Montague and Juliet of the house of Capulet had never seen each other before, but when they met, it was evident that they were in love. Their strong feelings for each other come across in the beauty of Shakespeare's words. Romeo remarks at seeing Juliet for the first time,

"O, she doth teach the torches to burn bright!
It seems she hangs upon the cheek of night
Like a rich jewel in an Ethiop's ear—
Beauty too rich for us, for earth too dear!"

ROMEO AND JULIET

Juliet's thoughts after she had met Romeo capture also her deep love, love so compelling that she would even give up her name:

"O Romeo, Romeo! Wherefore art thou Romeo?
Deny thy father and refuse thy name!
Or, I thou wilt not, be but sworn my love,
And I'll no longer be a Capulet."

First love, even in Shakespeare's time, was perhaps the strongest emotion that young people feel. Almost every adult will refer back to their "first love" as immature, but nonetheless a love mixed with very strong feelings. Even older teenagers who have had the experience of "first love" may have "moved on" in their love lives, but they remember their "first love" as an experience that was often overpowering. The lesson of Romeo and Juliet's sudden love for each other is just how strong initial love tends to be. Young people who are in love for the first time must understand that even if it doesn't feel like it, most probably, there will be stronger loves that follow the first one. They must also be aware that the overpowering feeling of first love may cause the young couple to do and say things that will only hurt them in their future.

Preliminary Thought

1. **The meditation refers to the term "true love." Define your idea of "true love."**
2. **In your opinion, can there be "love at first sight"? Yes or no and why?**
3. **The meditation refers to some things that first love may cause for a young couple. What are some of the things that people in first love tend to do which will possibly hurt them in the future?**

Notes

ROMEO AND JULIET

Reflection/Ideas/Discussion

WHAT SCENE DURING THIS SESSION STRIKES YOU THE MOST AND WHY?

4. Scene analysis: The Montague and Capulet "gangs." What is the underlying reason why there are gangs in our larger cities? What can be done about it?
5. Scene analysis: Young people, including Romeo and Mercutio have fun. a) What is the principal source of fun for young people in your locale at the present time? b) If you had your way, what would you do to allow teenagers to have more fun in your locale?
6. Scene analysis: Romeo takes some kind of pill before he goes to the party. The action is not in the play and seems to indicate some type of drug to make him have a better time. What is the principal problem with taking illegal drugs by young people?
7. Scene analysis: Romeo and Juliet obviously fall in love with each other. It is the proverbial "love at first sight" which is the subject of the meditation for this session. In the play, Juliet is actually supposed to be only fourteen years old. Do you believe that in general, there can be "true love" when a person is a) 13-15 years old; b) 16-18 years old; c) 18-21 years old?
8. Dialogue analysis: Juliet speaks of her love for Romeo as "My only love, sprung from my only hate." Do you believe that families in general play so strong a part in a relationship that they can break it up? Yes or no and why?

Notes

ROMEO AND JULIET

SESSION II
[Corresponding to Shakespeare's Act II (middle) to Act III, Scene V (middle)]
From: : After Romeo and Juliet fall into the water.
To: After Romeo returns from banishment and Juliet takes off Romeo's shirt.
Approximate time: 39 minutes.

Theme: Acting in a rage often leads to doing things that we never really want to do.

Scripture: **Matthew 5:21-22** Jesus gives his teaching on anger.

Doctrine/Application
[*Catechism of the Catholic Church* reference: numbers 2302-2303]

During this session of "Romeo and Juliet," the usually gentle, love-seeking Romeo gives into a rage that suddenly possesses him because of what happens to his good friend Mercutio. After he gives into his rage, Director Luhrmann in the movie focuses on the horror that Romeo feels. It becomes evident that Romeo did not want to do what he did. Acting in a rage often leads to doing things that were never intended. In particular here, Romeo discovers that his angry action has changed his whole life.

Jesus takes anger and rage to task in his Sermon on the Mount. "You have heard...`You shall not kill,'...but I say to you, whoever is angry with his brother will be liable to judgment." (Matthew 5:21-22) Incredibly, Jesus compares the act of anger to the act of killing another, saying to his followers that acting out vengeance toward another is the same as murder of another. Jesus felt strongly about anger.

Why? Probably because of the interior havoc that this awful emotion can wreak. Robert Green Ingersoll once wrote that "Anger blows out the lamp of the mind." Angry people tend to lose control, and destroy, at least momentarily, any positive sensitivity toward themselves or others.

Unfortunately, we personally know of many examples of anger. Angry parents cause fear and terror among their children. Angry children say things to parents that they wish they never would have said. People in anger can destroy in one minute friendships that took years to build. Families and communities are purposely torn apart by people who act out of an inner anger that controls their every action.

Once anger is upon us in all its ferocity, it seems to be almost impossible to manage. Romeo discovers this unfortunate truth in this session of "Romeo and Juliet." Viewed as a force of nature, anger is like real fire, which if you can catch it in time, can be extinguished. However, once the fire is well started, there is almost nothing that will stop it.

ROMEO AND JULIET

So, after listening carefully to Jesus' words, what do sincere Christians do about their anger? Simply put, they must learn to recognize the general and immediate circumstances that loosen the backdraft of rage within them and then proceed to do something about it.

The only way we can grow spiritually is through self-knowledge. It is also the only way to reduce our anger.

Preliminary Thought

9. How is anger like murder?
10. The meditation says that "Angry people tend to lose control, and destroy, at least momentarily, any positive sensitivity toward themselves or others." Describe an instance which describes the truth of the statement.
11. What are the best ways to acquire self-knowledge?

Notes

Reflection/Ideas/Discussion

WHAT SCENE DURING THIS SESSION STRIKES YOU THE MOST AND WHY?

ROMEO AND JULIET

12. Scene analysis: Juliet will not allow their love activity to reach the point of total physical love because they have not yet vowed marriage. For the Christian, it is refreshing to see a couple refusing to have sex before marriage. a) Do you think that this scene will help young people stay away from premarital sex? b) What is the best reason for young people to stay away from premarital sex?
13. Romeo and Juliet engage in "love activity": a) Granted there are many scenes of nudity in movies (one of them coming up in this movie), but do you think that even this type of activity where there is no nudity is too explicit for movies? Yes or no and why? b) Do you think your parents would agree with your answer? Yes or no and why?
14. Scene analysis: Romeo and Juliet marry each other. a) Specifically, should Fr. Lawrence have married them given the circumstances? Yes or no and why? b) Generally speaking, how much preparation time should be spent before the two get married? c) Do you believe young people are marrying too young these days? Yes or no and why? d) In your opinion, what are the three most important elements which must be present for a happy marriage? e) Shakespeare has Fr. Lawrence say "Love moderately." What do you think is the meaning of his words?
15. Scene analysis: Romeo does not want to fight, nor does he want Mercutio to fight. a) Why did he not want to fight? b) Do you think that it is always a cowardly thing to back down from a fight? Yes or no and why?
16. Scene analysis: The circumstances of Mercutio's death. Tybalt takes advantage of Mercutio as Romeo restrains Mercutio. a) Do you think that you would have behaved the way Romeo did after Mercutio was killed? Yes or no and why? b) Specifically, do you think it was morally correct for Romeo to kill Tybalt? Yes or no and why? c) Can you construe what Romeo did as "self-defense"? Yes or no and why?

Notes

ROMEO AND JULIET

SESSION III
[Corresponding to Shakespeare's Act III, Scene V (middle) to Act V, Scene III]
From: After Romeo returns from banishment and Juliet takes off Romeo's shirt.
To: End.
Approximate time: 36 minutes.

Theme: Passionate love can take away our reason.

Scripture: **1 Corinthians 7:21-24** Paul warns his readers not to become slaves to others.

Doctrine/Application
[*Catechism of the Catholic Church* **reference:** numbers 2346-2350]

When Paul the Apostle urges his Corinthian readers not be become slaves to other human beings, he did not have the 1990 dating patterns of North America in mind. But he could have spoken no better words for some of the situations which are common to modern lovers.

Unfortunately, as one begins a dating relationship, or even more commonly, as people discover the inner workings of choosing a possible partner for life, such a possibility exists. We may indeed choose to be slaves to other human beings, especially when we become so in love that we do not allow our reasoning to function. Such people are in love with love, and they will allow nothing to stand in the way of their feelings. The ultimate example, of course, is suicide because the lover reasons that there is no longer any reason to live.

William Shakespeare called his "Romeo and Juliet" a tragedy because of that very reason. Romeo and Juliet both reasoned that they simply could not live without the other. The fact is that at some particular moment we may be so disappointed that we do not desire to live, but moments change. There will be another particular moment, and we will see just how blind we were when we were controlled by strong feelings. "A person in passion," the old saying goes, "rides a mad horse."

People who have been hurt because of a love relationship, no matter what the circumstances of the hurt, must give themselves time to think things over. A cool head must make significant decisions, especially if those decisions involve permanency. Because we are slaves to no other human being, we can allow no other human being to control us and our feelings. St. Paul says very well: "The slave called in the Lord is a freed person in the Lord." It is a statement Romeo and Juliet should have heard. It is also a statement every lover should hear.

ROMEO AND JULIET

> **Preliminary Thought**
>
> 17. What do you think are the signs that people are in "love with love," that is, that they are "a slave" to their lover?
> 18. If you have a friend who is close to suicide because of a love relationship which has ceased for some reason, what is the best thing you can do for her/him?
> 19. Do you think that young people often allow others to control them and their feelings? Yes or no and why?

Notes

> **Reflection/Ideas/Discussion**
>
> **WHAT SCENE DURING THIS SESSION STRIKES YOU THE MOST AND WHY?**
> 20. Scene analysis: Juliet's father and Juliet fight. There is little doubt that parents as strong as Juliet's father will significantly affect a young person growing up. When such verbal (and sometimes) physical abuse happens to the young person, what should he/she do?
> 21. Scene analysis: Juliet's mother refuses to help her. a) Do you think that a wife should ever reverse a husband's decision? Yes or no and why? b) Do you think that a husband should ever reverse a wife's decision? Yes or no and why? c) Do you think that either a husband or wife should have more control of their children than the other? Yes or no and why?

ROMEO AND JULIET

22. Scene analysis: Romeo sees the fulfillment of an earlier dream. Do you think that there is such a thing as people having dreams that predict the future? Yes or no and why?
23. Scene analysis: The double suicide. This is the subject of the meditation for this session of the movie. Romantic love often takes away our reasoning power. a) What is the most important lesson that can be learned after studying this unfortunate set of events? b) Do you think that a young person can be affected by loss of love so much as to commit suicide? Yes or no and why?
24. Scene analysis: As you study the Montague and Capulet families, do you think that there is any hope of reconciliation? Yes or no and why?
25. Analysis: a) What is the most important lesson to be learned in the tragedy of "Romeo and Juliet"? b) After you have determined what it is, how does it apply to modern times?

Further Material

ROMEO AND JULIET

SHINE

GENERAL THEME

Much of the time, adults are the way they are because of their early lives.

SESSION I
From: Begins right away.
To: After Dr. Rosen talks through the closed door to Peter who is hiding, saying "He's not ready," and walks away.
Approximate time: 34 minutes.

Theme: The influence of a father on a growing person is enormous.

Scripture: **Matthew 2:19-23** Joseph was a true father to Jesus.

Doctrine/Application
[*Catechism of the Catholic Church* reference: number 2221-2224]

Anyone who knows what it is like to raise children understands completely the volumes that are contained in the one sentence from Matthew's Gospel: "[Joseph and his family] went and dwelt in a town called Nazareth." (Matthew 2:23) Unwritten in this verse are all of the normal elements of raising a child: the care, the instruction about religion, the education into a trade, the correction, the guiding, the offering of advice, and so forth. Jesus was God, but Jesus also had to grow through the usual moments of infancy, adolescence and young adulthood. As Matthew in particular points out in his "Infancy Section" of chapters one and two of his Gospel, Jesus' foster father, Joseph, played an enormous role in Jesus' growth and beliefs.

Peter Helfgott was the father of David, a young genius in the art of playing the piano. He could have been very good for David, so helpful, so supportive, and so able to direct him in the development of his talent. David was open to his direction, open to his love, and desirous of anything his father could give him. David loved his father and wanted to be loved by him. All the circumstances were such that David Helfgott could have been a concert pianist of the highest quality. But his father was not what he should have been. As we view the first session of the movie "Shine," we can try to identify his problem with descriptions such as "too concerned about himself" or "jealous of his son's talent" or "tyrannical in running his family." But whatever description we may use, Peter had an enormous influence on David, and it was not a good one.

SHINE

Child abuse is rampant in our society. There are many names for it, and many descriptions of it. But always, the ultimate cause is in the mind of the adult. The child is completely helpless, completely vulnerable. We easily see that portrayed during this first session of the movie. David not only wanted his father's wholesome love; he was open to receive it in whatever way it came. The unfortunate reality was that not only did Peter not give his son the love David needed, but his father also was acting out his own problems on the whole family, and therefore on David.

Every father should carefully watch the movie "Shine." In fact, every young man, and woman, for that matter, must see the effect of parenting or lack of parenting in our society. Perhaps, if they do, they will understand clearly how important a sane, functioning parent is to a child.

Preliminary Thought

1. The Gospels say little about Joseph. As you think of what he did as foster father, what do you think was his greatest virtue? Why?
2. a) What is the most important thing that a father should do for his family? b) In particular, that a father should do for his children?
3. What is the worst form of child abuse that you can think of? Why did you choose the one you did?
4. In your opinion, do you think *most* fathers raise their children well in today's society? Yes or no and why?

Notes

SHINE

Reflection/Ideas/Discussion

WHAT SCENE DURING THIS SESSION STRIKES YOU THE MOST AND WHY?

5. Scene analysis: How the "sane" adults act around David. Do you believe that we act well around people who are mentally unstable? Yes or no and why?
6. Scene analysis: David walks home with his Dad. Note that he walks behind his Dad. What, if anything, does this indicate about their relationship?
7. Scene analysis: Peter, David's father, makes David repeat the words: "I'm a very lucky boy." What, if anything, does this indicate about the father?
8. Scene analysis: Peter obviously runs the household with an iron hand. Is there anything that could have been done to help him see what he was doing? Yes or no and why?
9. Dialogue analysis: Peter says to David: "One day you will make me very proud." Selfishness is portrayed here. a) Do you believe that selfishness plays too big a role as parents deal with their young children? Yes or no and why? b) In what way have you seen parents show selfishness when they were dealing with their children?
10. Character analysis: David's mother. How would you describe David's mother as you have seen her portrayed in the movie?
11. Scene analysis: The young girl talks to David. Why did David's father not like the interaction?
12. Scene analysis: Peter decides that David will not go to America to study. Why did he make such a decision?
13. Scene analysis: In the bathroom, Peter beats David. This is clearly child abuse. What, if anything could David have done differently?

Notes

SHINE

SESSION II

From: After Dr. Rosen talks through the closed door to Peter who is hiding, saying "He's not ready," and walks away.

To: After receiving David's phone call, Peter stares out into the rain, and slams the blind.

Approximate time: 33 minutes.

Theme: Young people must find their own way at some time in their lives.

Scripture: **Matthew 12: 46-50** Jesus shows that nothing can stand in the way of his ministry.

Doctrine/Application
[*Catechism of the Catholic Church* **reference:** number 2230]

If people read this Scripture passage the wrong way, they might construe it as an insult. Jesus seems to ignore Mary and his brothers, saying, "Who is my mother? Who are my brothers? And stretching out his hand toward his disciples, he said, 'Here are my mother and my brothers.'" (Matthew 12:48-49) But if people read the passage as Jesus meant it, namely, with the thought of what is the most important part in his life after he had left his home, his answer rings true. His ministry is the most important thing in his life. Yes, parents and family are still important, but everyone must find their own way at some time in their lives, and Jesus' way was the obligation, as he saw it, to preach the kingdom.

When parents block their young people from developing well, especially in the case of the young adults who are about to go out on their own into the world, they are abusing their children. Children have the right to grow, and part of the growth must be the chance to try life on their own. Parents who leave the apron strings attached to their young adults can easily harm their offspring's futures.

Peter Helfgott did not believe that. In his mind, he was the father of the family, and when the father of the family spoke, everyone should listen, especially the children. And if they did not, there would be hell to pay. As he lived out that belief, the audience of the movie "Shine" can easily see how he was wrong, and what effect it had on David, his son, especially after his son had established his own independence.

SHINE

> **Preliminary Thought**
>
> 14. Do you think that Jesus showed disrespect toward Mary and his brothers in answering the way he did? Yes or no and why?
> 15. At what age do you think young adults are old enough "to make it in the world"? Give reason for your answer.
> 16. What attitude should young people have toward their parents after the young people leave their home? Discuss your answer.

Notes

> **Reflection/Ideas/Discussion**
>
> **WHAT SCENE DURING THIS SESSION STRIKES YOU THE MOST AND WHY?**
>
> 17. Scene analysis: Peter makes up with David. It is only on Peter's terms, "shaming" David into loving him. What do you find wrong in this scene and dialogue?
> 18. Scene analysis: David does not win the National contest. What principal effect did the loss have on David?
> 19. Analysis: David's friendship with Katharine Susannah Pritchard. What did the friendship mean to David? To Mrs. Pritchard?
> 20. Scene analysis: Peter and David violently disagree with each other concerning David's desire to go to the Royal College of London. This is the scene referred to in the meditation in which David declares his independence. What was most striking about the scene for you?

SHINE

> 21. Scene analysis: David obviously is becoming more and more nervous with very strange behavior while he is away at school (e.g., wearing only a shirt while he is getting his mail). In your opinion, what are the causes of it?
> 22. Scene analysis: Katharine Pritchard dies. What effect do you think this had on David?
> 23. Scene analysis: Director Scott Hicks uses the piece by Rachmaninoff as a culminating point of David's mental breakdown. Why do you think this specific piece and the performance of it caused his breakdown?
> 24. Scene analysis: Peter refuses to answer David when David calls him on the phone. In your opinion, do you think that the majority of fathers would treat their sons this way? Yes or no and why?

Notes

SESSION III

From: After receiving David's phone call, Peter stares out into the rain, and slams the blind.

To: End.

Approximate time: 35 minutes.

Theme: People can lead fulfilled lives if they feel loved.

Scripture: **Luke 7:36-50** Jesus pardons a sinful woman.

Doctrine/Application
[*Catechism of the Catholic Church* reference: number 1828-1829]

As one studies David Helfgott's life in the movie "Shine," and especially the effects of the abuse by his father Peter, one cannot help but be struck by the true love which David finally received later on in his life. The abuse caused David to have

SHINE

severe difficulties with his life, but those who loved him brought about a time when he could finally "shine." In particular, one must study the love that Beryl Alcott had for David. Hers was an unconditional love that allowed David to finally lead the fulfilled life that he deserved to lead.

Her love was not unlike the love Jesus showed the sinful woman in Luke's Gospel. As Jesus interacts with the Pharisees, telling them a parable about forgiveness when people ask for it, he not only forgives the woman her sins. He also leads her to a peace that she had probably never felt before she met this wonderful man. Jesus' display of unconditional love for the woman gave her the sense of fulfillment that she had always wanted with her life. (Luke 7:50)

The lesson of Beryl Alcott and Jesus Christ is not a difficult one to comprehend. However, it is difficult to imitate. We Christians must recognize more and more the effects of Jesus' directive to love our neighbor. If we do, more and more people will be able to lead fulfilled lives. Love is the necessary condition for lives to be wholesome.

Preliminary Thought

25. What are the characteristics of "unconditional love"?
26. What are the necessary conditions for one to receive "forgiveness" from God?
27. Do you believe that most Christians have totally accepted the doctrine of Jesus that we must love our neighbor? Yes or no and why?

Notes

SHINE

Reflection/Ideas/Discussion

WHAT SCENE DURING THIS SESSION STRIKES YOU THE MOST AND WHY?

28. Scene analysis: David in the mental hospital. What do you think are the main characteristics of people who work in mental hospitals?
29. Scene analysis: Beryl Alcott takes David in. What do you think was her main motivation?
30. Scene analysis: Peter goes to David. a) Why did he finally go to David? b) How do you think David felt as his father came back to him?
31. Scene analysis: Gillian begins to care about David. What do you think her motivation was as she began to care for him?
32. Scene analysis: David and Gillian marry. Obviously, Gillian must "give" more to the relationship. Do you think she married David out of compassion more than anything else? Yes or no and why?
33. Scene analysis: David plays the concert and is appreciated at the end, thanks to the encouragement of Gillian. Finally he has a chance to "shine." What kind of a future do you think David will have?
34. Dialogue/scene analysis: At Peter's tomb. David does not seem to show any hatred toward his father. He only says, "Life goes on." Why do you think David does not show any emotion at his father's death?
35. What is the one lesson to remember after watching the movie "Shine"?

Further Material

SLEEPERS

[This film is rated R by the motion picture industry because of language and a brief scene of nudity. It is recommended for older young people only.]

GENERAL THEME

The wounds of childhood not only carry through life, but they direct our actions unless we control them.

SESSION I

From: Begins after the title "Sleepers" which follows the initial list of actors.
To: After Shakes says in his narrative, "As for rehabilitation, forget it," and after the scene in the woodworking shop.
Approximate time: 36 minutes.

Theme: The circumstances in which a child grows up including family and neighborhood affect that child's life forever.

Scripture: **Luke 8:49-55** Jesus is concerned about a child.

Doctrine/Application
[*Catechism of the Catholic Church* reference: numbers 2221-2226]

Jesus knew about children. He knew that they needed all the help they could get. And so, he reminded the parents of the child that he had just cured that they should give her something to eat. (Luke 8:55) One surmises that Jesus was well aware that if the environment in which a child lived was not healthy, the child could easily be hurt.

The four friends who initially felt that they ruled the West Side of Manhattan-- Tommy, John, Michael and Lorenzo (or Shakes)--grew up in a very harmful atmosphere. Such is the setting of the movie "Sleepers." The boys generally did not have parents who cared; their adult role models were often abusive to them, both physically and verbally; and the adults who did care about them were drowned out by a daily life that was too concerned about money and how to put food on the table.

Children are vulnerable. As one views the first session of "Sleepers," one cannot help escape the feeling that because of the way they grew up, the four boys were going to fall into trouble. It is an important lesson for any adult who has the responsibility of raising children in the world in which we live. It is also an important lesson for older young people who realize what they have come through already in their lives. They can realize what the circumstances of their lives have brought and react appropriately.

SLEEPERS

If the circumstances were good, it may mean that they will enter adult lives with a good foundation or unfortunately, if the circumstances were not good, it may mean that they will have to understand the problems they have inherited, and change before they grow older.

Preliminary Thought

1. In general, from your understanding of the Gospels, how do you think Jesus felt about children?
2. a) In general, on a scale of 1-10 where 10 is high, how much effect will a family which is not a good family have on a child? b) In general, using the same scale, how much effect will a harmful environment, like a ghetto slum area have? c) In general, do you think that a good family can "off-set" a rough environment as a child grows? Yes or no and why?
3. If a child grows up in a bad atmosphere with a bad home life, and has not turned out well, do you think that such a young person who has made it into high school can change things for the better during high school? Yes or no and why?

Notes

Reflections/Ideas/Discussion

WHAT SCENE DURING THIS SESSION STRIKES YOU THE MOST AND WHY?

SLEEPERS

4. Scene analysis: Shakes' father beats his mother. a) In today's world, do you think that there is much wife abuse? Yes or no and why? b) Do you believe that the Church should change its rules about divorce? Yes or no and why?
5. Analysis: Why did the Church not have more effect on the boys, given that they went to a Catholic school and were often servers at Mass?
6. Character analysis: Fr. Bobby. a) Evidently, Fr. Bobby was a good person, one that the boys respected. What characteristics should a priest have? b) In your opinion, what is the reason for the priestly vocation shortage in the Roman Catholic Church?
7. Scene analysis: King Benny and his background. Mafia-connected, King Benny now went about a respectable life that was still part of a "Mafia scene." In your opinion, how is one's life affected by a "Mafia connection"?
8. Scene analysis: Shakes' early job is part of King Benny's activity. What do you think this would do to the mind of a young boy?
9. Scene analysis: Michael "helps" the girl in the wheelchair by losing the game. What are the best ways for young people to help other young people?
10. Scene analysis: Shakes goes to Fr. Bobby after the hot dog vender incident. Is there anything else Fr. Bobby could have or should have done? Yes or no and why?
11. Dialogue/scene analysis: Nokes, the guard, makes fun of the religious scapular around Shakes' neck. What was your feeling at the scene and why?

Notes

SESSION II

From: After Shakes says in his narrative, "As for rehabilitation, forget it," and after the scene in the woodworking shop.

To: As Shakes and Michael are talking about the plan, and Michael says, "No, it will play better in court if they don't know."

Approximate time: 37 minutes.

SLEEPERS

Theme: When someone suffers a devastating evil because of someone else, the feeling of human nature is toward revenge.

Scripture: **John 7:45-52** Jealousy blinds the religious leaders and directs them toward revenge.

Doctrine/Application
[*Catechism of the Catholic Church* reference: number 2262]

People who have only read about the evil shown in the movie "Sleepers," can never really understand it. But when it is part of everyday living over the year, it forever affects the psyche of those who suffer it. The four boys who once in their opinion, ruled the West Side of Manhattan would forever remember the atrocities that they experienced at the Wilkinson Home for Boys. Any observer of the situation could easily understand their natural desire for revenge.

The circumstances and situation of Jesus' time were nothing like the incredible horror the boys of Wilkinson suffered, but the Pharisee's desire for revenge had the same intensity. The Pharisees felt that they were wronged. This man Jesus had deliberately led the people against them. What he was doing was so wrong that it could be compared to hatred of God's Law. Such disrespect for God's Law naturally led them to get back at Jesus and the desire blinded them when anyone tried to reason otherwise. Such is the evil of revenge. (John 7:45-52)

Whether based in truth or not, revenge is a force to be reckoned with. The person who feels revenge must be in control enough to measure what it could possibly cause and what direction it may lead one's life. If people are not in control, the revenge will control them, and the end result may be much worse than any previous evil.

Preliminary Thought

12. As you have studied what the four boys have suffered so far at the Wilkinson Home for Boys, what are some comparable situations in today's world?
13. What is the real evil connected with revenge?
14. Do you believe it is true that revenge can be worse than even the evil that caused it? Yes or no and why?

SLEEPERS

Notes

Reflections/Ideas/Discussion

WHAT SCENE DURING THIS SESSION STRIKES YOU THE MOST AND WHY?

15. Scene analysis: The sexual abuse of the young boys. What is the principal reason why this is so wrong?
16. Dialogue analysis: Fr. Bobby tells Shakes not to let the reform school "kill" him. What do you think he meant?
17. Scene analysis: The football game. The boys were "free" for ninety minutes. What do you think they mean by "being free" and was it a good thing for them?
18. Scene analysis: The four boys discuss what to do. Was their reasoning correct? Was there anything anyone could have done? Yes or no and why?
19. Scene analysis: Tommy and John thirteen years after Wilkinson. They are now murderers and abusers of alcohol and drugs. What do you think are the principal reasons why they have chosen such a direction?
20. Scene analysis: Tommy and John kill Nokes: the ultimate revenge. Did it serve the purpose they wanted it to serve? Yes or no and why?
21. Scene analysis: Michael wants "to finish it." Do you think that people can ever finish the feeling of revenge? Yes or no and why?

Notes

SLEEPERS

SESSION III

From: As Shakes and Michael are talking about the plan, and Michael says, "No, it will play better in court if they don't know."

To: After King Benny says to Shakes: "You're a nice kid; you always were. Don't let this change it."

Approximate time: 37 minutes.

Theme: Revenge is extremely difficult to control, and when it is done with pre-meditation, it may affect the people involved forever.

Scripture: **Matthew 5:38-42** Jesus teaches about revenge.

Doctrine/Application

[*Catechism of the Catholic Church* reference: number 2261-2262]

One assumes that Michael and Shakes, along with Tommy and John, had heard the words of Jesus in the Sermon on the Mount: "I say to you, offer no resistance to one who is evil." (Matthew 5:39) They had attended Catholic school; they had served many Masses. Why had it not sunk in?

It leads one to the question of whether there is ever a time when the rule of Jesus does not apply? In fact, could there be a time when the only rule of action must be a revengeful one? As the viewer of the movie "Sleepers" senses what went on in the Wilkinson Home for Boys, the possibility of revenge toward the guards may be the only way that the young men who suffered the atrocities could even live a decent life again.

Is that true, or is it more true that the pre-meditated act of revenge which Michael and Shakes perpetrated actually hurt them more than even the horrors of their youth? No doubt there were many reasons why the lives of the boys of the movie "Sleepers" were affected forever. It is conceivable that the feeling of revenge and the hatred connected with it could have been one of the principal reasons for their shattered lives.

SLEEPERS

Jesus' words concerning revenge are not easy, especially in a case like the one portrayed in the movie, but they may suggest even more than the highest religious thought. They may be words that can actually heal a psychologically troubled soul. Young people and in fact, all people, must consider what their thinking is doing to their behavior. Revenge can easily dictate behavior and thought which will harm a person forever.

Preliminary Thought

22. Why are there so many cases where solid ideals given early in life do not have any effect later on?
23. Answer the suggested question of the meditation: "Is there ever a time when the rule of Jesus concerning revenge does not apply?" Yes or no and why?
24. Do you agree with the assertion of the meditation that desire for and carrying out of revenge can harm a person forever? Yes or no and why?

Notes

Reflection/Ideas/Discussion

WHAT SCENE DURING THIS SESSION STRIKES YOU THE MOST AND WHY?

25. Analysis: What is the significance of the word "Sleepers" which is the word used on the street for someone who spent time in a juvenile detention center?
26. Scene analysis: Carol refers to Michael "shutting down" with respect to pursuing a relationship. What are the principal reasons why it is so difficult for one who has suffered sexual abuse to love?

SLEEPERS

> 27. Scene analysis: Shakes and his dad. In your opinion, is there ever a possibility that his dad could understand what he has done to his family. Yes or no and why?
> 28. Scene analysis: Shakes prays his rosary and has flashbacks to what happened. Given the circumstances, should prayer be able to help in this situation? Yes or no and why?
> 29. Dialogue analysis: Shakes tells Fr. Bobby that "saving two of his boys" is not the same as "lying." Do you agree? Yes or no and why?
> 30. Scene analysis: Did Shakes behave in a morally correct manner as he took out revenge on the guard who had turned into a drug dealer? Yes or no and why?
> 31. Scene analysis: Carol meets Michael on the subway train, saying to him that if he would have told her about the abuse, things could have been different. Do you agree? Yes or no and why?

Notes

SESSION IV

From: After King Benny says to Shakes: "You're a nice kid; you always were. Don't let this change it."

To: End.

Approximate time: 34 minutes.

Theme: People are more important than law.

Scripture: **Romans 13:8-10** The only obligation we have is to love one another.

SLEEPERS

Doctrine/Application
[*Catechism of the Catholic Church* reference: numbers 1970-1971]

In the movie "Sleepers," Father Bobby found himself in a position where he could truly help two of his boys. As he told them many times, there was nothing that he would not do for them. He wanted to keep them out of trouble, he wanted to give them the chance for a good future. He had been instrumental in helping them through childhood, now--from what he could see of their futures anyway-- he had the chance to help them be good adults. But in order to do it, he would have to lie. In fact, he would have to commit perjury.

Is there ever a time when moral people can directly violate the law of the land and still be committed to the principles of morality that they have freely accepted? Case in point: is there ever a time when a priest who has vowed to remain obedient to the Roman Catholic Church and its laws, can lie directly under oath in a court of law?

If the answer to those questions would be in the affirmative, it would not be too difficult to find justification in the writings of Paul. Paul had a difficult time with the Hebrew Law which he had once defended so strongly. He felt that it had done harm in the eyes of God because it had led people to overlook things that were perhaps more important. "Owe nothing to anyone," Paul writes, "except to love one another; for the one who loves another has fulfilled the law." (Romans 13:8)

If the answer were in the negative, namely that Fr. Bobby should first of all find that he had the moral obligation to tell only the truth, he could also find justification in the writings of Paul. Fr. Bobby would judge in that case, as so many have in similar situations, that the punishment would teach a lesson--ultimately, a lesson of love-- that was much more valuable than the temporary freedom which might come from his judgment of conscience.

No matter what his decision, there is no doubt that law--the law of the Church, the written law of some code--is important. But there is also no doubt that the law does not cover every situation. When a person judges with good reason that the law would hurt people, then the law has lost its reason for existence. However, law is never to be discarded lightly. The law truly can still serve people if people are more important than law.

Preliminary Thought

32. In your opinion, is there ever a situation that would allow for perjury? Yes or no and why?

SLEEPERS

> 33. What would you do in Fr. Bobby's case?
> 34. Do you believe that too often people give into a weak conscience and disobey the law? Yes or no and why?

Notes

> **Reflection/Ideas/Discussion**
>
> **WHAT SCENE DURING THIS SESSION STRIKES YOU THE MOST AND WHY?**
> 35. Scene analysis: Little Caesar kills Addison. Obviously, this was not the morally correct way to take care of this situation. What would have been a better way?
> 36. Scene analysis: Ferguson's testimony. Obviously, Michael wanted Ferguson to finally admit what happened at Wilkinson. Was this a good way to do it? Was there a better way to accomplish it?
> 37. Dialogue/scene analysis: Defense lawyer Synder questions how a good man and friend could abuse the young boys he was paid to look after. In your opinion, why did Ferguson not do anything about it when he was at Wilkinson with Nokes?
> 38. Dialogue analysis: King Benny tells Shakes that the street is all that matters; God is for uptown people. What did he mean, and is it true?
> 39. Scene analysis: Fr. Bobby's testimony. What is your feeling about what Fr. Bobby did and why?

SLEEPERS

40. Analysis: What do you think of Shakes' analysis that Fr. Bobby not only lied for Tommy and John, but he was testifying against Wilkinson Home for Boys and the evil that was there?
41. [Analysis: Constant reference is made to the book, *The Count of Monte Cristo*, and in particular to the revenge portrayed. The instructor may want to make a comparison of some sort.]
42. Analysis: Obviously Tommy and John could have led better lives, but did not. In your opinion, what would have had to happen in order to make them follow a different course?
43. Analysis: The disclaimers at the end of the film. a) Do you believe what the New York State Youth Division said? Yes or no and why? b) Do you believe what the District Attorney's Office of Manhattan said? Yes or no and why?
44. Analysis: What is the one lesson from the movie "Sleepers" that every young person could learn?

Further Material

SLEEPERS

SPEED 2: CRUISE CONTROL

GENERAL THEME

We must be courageous, even in the face of severe difficulties.

SESSION I
From: Begins right away.
To: After Geiger tells Mr. Juliano, "See what you made me do."
Approximate time: 40 minutes.

Theme: Learning how to communicate is the most difficult part of preparing for marriage.

Scripture: **Matthew 5:33-37** Jesus speaks about the importance of open communication.

Doctrine/Application
[*Catechism of the Catholic Church* **reference:** numbers 1603-1605]

Jesus was talking against the necessity of taking oaths when he said "Let your 'yes' mean 'yes' and your 'no' mean 'no.'" (Matthew 5: 37) But his words can easily be applied to speech between people who are working on a possible marital relationship. If two people are building a deep love relationship, their "yes" and "no" to each other must imply much self revelation and no hiding. In fact, although the Bible does not mention it specifically, nor the catechisms of the church, the key to a good relationship is good communication.

In fact, in order to be fully human, and unquestionably, in order to encounter each other in marriage, we must learn the art of when and how to reveal the "mystery" of our inner selves. Most of us make only a weak response to the invitation of encounter with others because we feel uncomfortable in exposing our nakedness as persons. Some of us are willing only to pretend to do it, choosing to remain hidden; some find the courage to be completely open to others. Truly loving relationships only exist in the latter category.

Striving to be completely open to others is the foundation for any marriage preparation. The first part of the movie "Speed 2:Cruise Control" has very little to do with the action that will follow in the next two sessions. What is portrayed is primarily a struggle of discovering the communication patterns between two people who are about to be married.   Alex and Annie are two totally different people and their

SPEED 2: CRUISE CONTROL

communication patterns are not at all good as we start the movie presentation. The overall theme suggested for the film concerns itself with facing severe difficulties. It was made with the thought of the two sessions which follow, but perhaps the severe difficulty of discovering communication is much more important for the general public. Marriage can never be taken lightly, and communication between the two who will be married, no matter how difficult and how much time it takes to develop, is the most important part of marriage.

Preliminary Thought

1. **Do you agree with the meditation's thought that we must reveal ourselves completely to our spouses? Yes or no and why?**
2. **[The instructor may want to refer to a book like "Why Am I Afraid To Tell You Who I Am" by John Powell, S.J. for this question.] As you consider communication in marriage, what are the different levels of communication that you can think of?**
3. **The meditation says that "Most of us make only a weak response to the invitation of encounter with others because we feel uncomfortable in exposing our nakedness as persons." Do you find the statement to be true or false and why?**

Notes

Reflection/Ideas/Discussion

WHAT SCENE DURING THIS SESSION STRIKES YOU THE MOST AND WHY?

SPEED 2: CRUISE CONTROL

4. Scene analysis: Annie complains to Alex that he lied to her about what kind of a policeman he was. As you consider the necessity of revealing yourself to your future spouse, do you believe that there are certain things that can be held back from him/her? Yes or no and why?
5. Analysis: The cruise ship. Do you believe that in general Americans have a tendency of enjoying themselves *too* much? Yes or no and why?
6. Character analysis: Geiger. Obviously, the man is mentally unstable. He is also presented as thoroughly evil. Do you believe that such evil really exists in our world? Yes or no and why?
7. Scene analysis: Alex and Drew exchange glances. Obviously, Alex is concerned about Drew's handicap of not being able to speak except through sign language. In general, do young people treat other young people with disabilities or handicaps in a Christian way? Yes or no and why?
8. Dialogue analysis: Annie and Alex fight, saying that "we don't even know each other." What are the two or three most necessary elements of getting to know each other better?
9. Scene analysis: Geiger kills the captain. Do you believe that such depictions of relatively "calm murders" have an influence on the American viewing public? Yes or no and why?

Notes

SESSION II

From: After Geiger tells Mr. Juliano, "See what you made me do."
To: As Alex prepares to go into the water after first officer tries to warn the tanker.
Approximate time: 39 minutes.

SPEED 2: CRUISE CONTROL

Theme: Greed can cause sickness in a person to such a degree that the person ceases caring for anyone or anything.

Scripture: **Matthew 19:23-26** Jesus speaks words to people who are rich.

Doctrine/Application
[*Catechism of the Catholic Church* **reference:** numbers 2536-2537]

In the movie "Speed 2: Cruise Control," evil is personified in the person of Geiger. He has no care for anyone or anything except himself. In today's world, there are not many people who would fall into the same category, but there is evidence of the same driving force. Greed, especially greed for the diamonds on board the ship, is one of the major driving forces for Geiger. Greed is a major problem in our world as well. It can cause sickness in people to such a degree that they lose sight of everything but the riches they desire. They define their love and happiness in terms of the riches. The clear truth that may be unwritten in our society, but fundamental at the same time, is that wealth is an answer to the problem of achieving the *good* things in life. And the good things in life will enable us to love and be happy.

Jesus Christ would have difficulty with such a manner of thinking. His view into human nature sensed that having riches will not aid our approach to eternal life. In fact, in his thinking, what might easily result from a desire for riches is too much of a concern for the very un-eternal life here on earth. Rich people tend to concentrate on themselves and make it difficult for their ears to hear about the importance of others, a central point in Jesus' doctrine. Why be concerned about others when *I'm* interested in how much I can get from them. Why be concerned about the poor and the helpless when they add nothing to *my* love and happiness.

What do we do as Christians? The desire to face the challenge is necessary; in fact, it may be half of the solution. Too many Christians simply ignore what Jesus says. They must face head on the radical nature of Jesus' words. "It will be hard," Jesus says, "for one who is rich to enter the kingdom of heaven." Consequently, Christians must listen closely to Jesus and then, turn to action. Actions such as striving for only the riches that are necessary for decent living or trying constantly to acknowledge the difference between "needs" and "wants" may be the beginning of the Christian understanding of riches and greed.

Geiger in the movie "Speed 2: Cruise Control" is a sick individual driven by greed. Could it be that Jesus understood such sickness, and wanted to give us the opportunity to understand it?

SPEED 2: CRUISE CONTROL

Preliminary Thought

10. In your opinion, what *would* be the answer of a rich person in the world to Jesus' statement that "it will be hard for one who is rich to enter the kingdom of heaven"?
11. Do you agree with the meditation that "rich people tend to concentrate on themselves"? Yes or no and why?
12. A high school counselor has made this comment about education today: "It seems that everything in our high schools and colleges is geared so that the young people will make a lot of money when they graduate." Do you agree with the statement? Yes or no and why?

Notes

Reflection/Ideas/Discussion

WHAT SCENE DURING THIS SESSION STRIKES YOU THE MOST AND WHY?

13. Scene analysis: Mr. Juliano who suddenly is in charge of the ship. Was there anything he could have done differently? Yes or no and why?
14. Scene analysis: Geiger goes to the diamonds. This session of the movie is devoted to his greed. How can greed be prevented in the lives of people?
15. Scene analysis: The heroism of Alex and Dante at the lifeboat scene. Discuss any heroism you have seen in your ordinary daily life.
16. Dialogue analysis: Annie tells Alex that he doesn't have to save the ship. It is a true statement, but a person who is dedicated to some cause will give totally of himself/herself. As far as possible, define what Alex's "cause" for existence is.

SPEED 2: CRUISE CONTROL

> **17. Scene analysis: Drew is trapped, and finally rescued. As far as you can see, given the circumstances, what, if anything, could she had done differently?**

Notes

SESSION III
From: As Alex prepares to go into the water after first officer tries to warn the tanker.
To: End.
Approximate time: 39 minutes.

Theme: Even though we can never control all of the tragedies that happen, we must be courageous in our approach to life, accepting what happens.

Scripture: **Luke 22:39-46** Jesus suffers his agony in the garden.

Doctrine/Application
[*Catechism of the Catholic Church* reference: number 1808]

The attraction of modern audiences to the film "Speed 2: Cruise Control" may be this final session in which all of the special effects and action take place. But, the ending is more than sophisticated computer technology, stunt people, and clever photography. It also conveys a message that is well worth exploring. We can never control tragedies from happening in our lives. But we can begin to understand them as acts of God in some way and courageously accept them in that light.

There is no thought of God in the movie, but there is evidence of the presence of God. We can see such presence even in the tragedies that happen. Perhaps one of the proofs of the existence of God's action in our world is that so many tragedies could have happened, but never did. In the case of the movie, we can speak of God's grace at work in Alex as he tries to do everything possible to save his life and the lives of

SPEED 2: CRUISE CONTROL

others, and succeeds, saving more people than anyone could have thought possible. In real life, we see evidence of God's action even in tragedy. A tornado in Florida should have killed more than it did. A jumbo jet somersaults down the runway of an airport in New York, bursting into flames, breaking in two, and yet almost half of the people walk away. The believer will look at the tragedies which happen and say, "Thank God" for the good things that happened in spite of the tragedy, while a non-believer will consider any tragedy a proof that God cannot exist.

Jesus knew that his Father was real, and when he realized the tragedy that was about to happen to him, he very humanly asked to have it taken away. When he understood further that it was by his Father's design, he accepted the pain, even though, as Luke remarks, "his sweat became like drops of blood" (Luke 22:44), so intense was his mental suffering. Tragedies were not easy to understand, even for Jesus Christ.

Because of the fact that we are human beings, we will all be involved in tragedies in one way or another. Such a thought can be overwhelmingly negative for the non-believer. But, for the believer, we can courageously accept tragedies, as difficult as it may be, knowing that God is always at work in bringing about good in spite of any evil.

Preliminary Thought

18. What are the most difficult kind of tragedies to understand? Does good ever come out of them?
19. What do you think is the reason for tragedy and pain in our world, and why does God allow it?
20. Do you agree that "God is always at work bringing about good" as the meditation says? Yes or no and why?

Notes

SPEED 2: CRUISE CONTROL

Reflection/Ideas/Discussion

WHAT SCENE DURING THIS SESSION STRIKES YOU THE MOST AND WHY?

21. Scene analysis: Alex risks his life to save the ship. Do you believe that in general, people love others enough to risk their lives for them? Yes or no and why?

22. Dialogue/scene analysis: The people on the ship realize that they are not going to stop. As spoken in the meditation, the tragedy is going to happen, and they fully understand it. At that point in the movie, was there anything different that could have been done? Yes or no and why?

23. Scene analysis: The ship destroys boats and houses, and kills people as it comes ashore. As mentioned in the meditation, these are tragedies, but not nearly as bad as it could have been. God's grace is at work here. Where do you see God's grace most at work in our world?

24. Scene analysis: The diamonds fall into the sea. Greed has caused all of the pain and suffering, and now no one will have any reward. Most probably the movie is showing the futility of doing anything for money and that there are more important things than money in the world. In your opinion, list in order the three most important things which are part of your world right now.

25. Analysis: Do you believe that "greed" is the biggest cause of crime in our world? Yes or no and why?

Further Material

STAR TREK: FIRST CONTACT

GENERAL THEME

Sometimes doing the right thing means giving everything we have.

SESSION I

From: Begins after credits.
To: After manual release to the engineering door breaks and Picard says "Perhaps we should just knock."
Approximate time: 35 minutes.

Theme: The evil in our world never rests, and therefore we must always fight it.

Scripture: **1 Peter 5:8-11** We must resist the devil.

Doctrine/Application
[*Catechism of the Catholic Church* reference: number 309-314]

The English translation for the Greek word used in the text of 1 Peter 5:8 is *devour*, that is to *eat up greedily*. It fittingly describes the exact attitude of evil in our world, or the devil, as 1 Peter addresses such evil. "Your opponent, the devil," the author of 1 Peter writes, "is prowling around like a roaring lion looking for someone to devour." (1 Peter 5:8) Evil will not rest. Every situation is open to it in one way or another, and the task of evil, if it can be addressed as such, is to never relax in its pursuit of something to harm.

In many ways, such a description is the perfect description of the Borg in the movie "Star Trek: First Contact." The Borg had already conquered thousands, and at the beginning of the movie, it is ready to conquer the Federation of Planets as well. In time, it comes into contact with Jean-Luc Picard and the crew of the starship "Enterprise." As with all evil, the Borg always wants more. The Borg, evil, will conquer all in its quest for satisfaction. Its statement to the conquered kingdoms is the ominous "Resistance is futile," and their intention is to dominate all. Evil can only be stopped if it is destroyed in some way.

But there is hope. The first letter of Peter assures the Christian that even though it looks as though the devil will devour everything, it is not the case. The Christian has reason to resist, and can constantly be assured of the presence of Jesus who will "restore, confirm, strengthen, and establish" once again. (1 Peter 5:10) Likewise, there is hope for the people of the Federation and the crew of the Enterprise even

STAR TREK: FIRST CONTACT

though it looks as though evil will have its day. Even as the Klingon Federated commander Worf says in this first session, "Maybe it is a good day to die," Captain Jean-Luc Picard realizes that he has "been there." He knows what being a Borg is all about, and he will be able to fight.

Preliminary Thought

1. a) Define "evil." b) What is most evil in our world today?
2. Referring to your answer in number 1, what "solution" if any, can you give for the evil mentioned?
3. The meditation asserts that even in the worst circumstances, there is hope. Why is this true for a Christian?
4. In the make-believe world of "Star Trek," what is most striking to you? Why?

Notes

Reflection/Ideas/Discussion

WHAT SCENE DURING THIS SESSION STRIKES YOU THE MOST AND WHY?

5. Scene analysis: Picard directly disobeys the Federation orders. In general, do the people of North America practice the virtue of obedience? Yes or no and why?
6. Scene analysis: Picard sees the necessity to follow the Borg back in time and repair what damage was done. Do you think that there is such a positive desire to do good and fight evil in our world at the present time? Yes or no and why?

STAR TREK: FIRST CONTACT

7. Scene analysis: The Enterprise blows up the Borg "sphere" as it fires on earth. There is much killing done in "Star Trek: First Contact" as there is in many movies today. a) Do you think all of the killing has any effect on us at all? b) In particular, what do very young people think as they watch all of the killing?
8. Dialogue/scene analysis: Data makes the comment that the nuclear missile was a weapon of war and now Cochran was going to introduce an era of peace with it. Do you think our world is ready to use nuclear weapons for peaceful purposes? Yes or no and why?
9. Scene analysis: The movie presents the inventor/scientist/innovator Zefran Cochran as an alcoholic and a weak personality. Do you think very many famous people had personal problems? Yes or no and why?
10. Dialogue/scene analysis: Picard tells Data to switch off his "emotion" chip. a) How important do you think emotions are in life? b) Specifically, would you want to "switch off your emotion chip" if you could? Yes or no and why?

Notes

SESSION II

From: After manual release to the engineering door breaks and Picard says "Perhaps we should just knock."

To: Immediately after the Borg throws Hawk over the edge of the Enterprise.

Approximate time: 36 minutes.

Theme: Peace can be achieved when people finally work together.

Scripture: **Luke 1:76-79** The Lord will lead us into the path of peace.

STAR TREK: FIRST CONTACT

Doctrine/Application
[*Catechism of the Catholic Church* **reference:** number 2302-2306]

Zechariah was speaking in prophecy as he spoke about his son, John, later to be called "the Baptist." He prophesied that John would go before the Lord to prepare his ways, and eventually guide everyone's feet into the path of peace. (Luke 1:76-79) He did not know exactly how that would be accomplished, but he knew that his son and the Lord who would follow him, would direct the world toward such a peace.

Unfortunately, the perfect peace which both John the Baptist and Jesus Christ wanted, has never found fulfillment. We study our history, and we necessarily must study war and the violation of peace. It is a clear fact that generally speaking, we are not prone to follow the path of peace.

Such a path is threatened by evil in the movie "Star Trek: First Contact." Evil or the Borg, as it is called in the movie, has managed to threaten all humankind both present and past, by taking over their freedom, and making everyone robots, so that free will is annihilated, or assimilated in its words. It is interesting to study the path of peace that had been achieved before that time. During this session, the crew of the Enterprise talk to someone who unwittingly will bring about such a peace. They tell him of what the "path of peace" will be. It will unite humanity. Poverty, disease, war—they are all conquered because finally people will be working together. In fact, even money is not needed since the acquisition of wealth is no longer a driving force in people's lives. Instead, people will be constantly trying to better themselves and the rest of humanity, no matter what the cost.

The belief that such a path of peace is worth fighting for is the conviction of Jean-Luc Picard and crew of the Enterprise. Although a fiction, it is a good guide for people of the world. If people really did work together, there would be no poverty, disease or war, and perhaps not even a need for money. It remains an ideal for humankind at the present time, but it is an ideal which every Christian should make a personal goal. Jesus has directed us to the path of peace; it is within our reach if we want it.

Preliminary Thought

11. If your country would "follow the path of peace," what would the leaders do first?
12. In your life right now, what does "the path of peace" consist of?
13. In your opinion, do the people of the world really "want" peace? Yes or no and why?

STAR TREK: FIRST CONTACT

Notes

Reflection/Ideas/Discussion

WHAT SCENE DURING THIS SESSION STRIKES YOU THE MOST AND WHY?

14. Scene analysis: Picard kills a crewman who is being assimilated by the Borg. This would correspond to our understanding of "mercy killing." Do you think that there is ever a time when someone can justify "mercy killing"? What is euthanasia? The Catholic Church believes that euthanasia is wrong. Why do you think they believe this way? [See *Catechism of the Catholic Church, nos. 2276-2279*]

15. Scene analysis: The "first contact" is with an alien nation, and after it is made, the universe is united. Do you believe that our universe could ever be united, even if an alien force tried to accomplish it? Yes or no and why?

16. Dialogue analysis: Picard tells Lily that first she must trust him. As a general rule, do we trust other human beings most of the time? Yes or no and why?

17. Dialogue/scene analysis: The Borg and Data talk. The Borg says that they assimilate other beings to bring about perfection. Is there any way that we can achieve perfection in the world? Yes or no and why?

18. Dialogue/scene analysis: Lily and Picard talk about money. Picard says that it does not exist in the 24th century, and the acquisition of wealth is no longer the driving force in people's lives. Do you think such a situation is possible where money does not play that much importance in the world? Yes or no and why?

19. Scene analysis: The Borg wants to assimilate the present and the future. Determine an evil at the present time that could compare to the Borg. What is the best way to stop this evil?

20. Scene analysis: Data is not "processed" to have emotions. If the world were run by logic and technology only, what would be the outcome?

STAR TREK: FIRST CONTACT

Notes

SESSION III
    From: Immediately after the Borg throws Hawk over the edge of the Enterprise.
    To: End.
    Approximate time: 34 minutes.

    Theme: When we understand the idea of sacrifice, we will understand what maturity is.

    Scripture: **Psalm 50:15-19**   The sacrifice we offer God must be a contrite spirit.

Doctrine/Application
[*Catechism of the Catholic Church* **reference:** number 2099-2100]
    If making a sacrifice can be defined in terms of giving up our personal preferences for the sake of a greater good, we see a number of "sacrifices" as the movie "Star Trek: First Contact" reaches its conclusion. During this session, we will witness the head-strong captain of the Enterprise, Jean-Luc Picard make sacrifices, in spite of his own desires. In order to accomplish a greater good, he discovers that he must sacrifice what he believes is right, and he is ready to make the ultimate sacrifice for his ship and his friend. Although things do not work out the way he thought, he makes the sacrifices, and is a better person because of it.
    Perhaps "becoming a better person" is what the psalmist meant as he addressed his God concerning sacrifice. "You are not pleased with sacrifices," the author of Psalm 50 writes, "should I offer a holocaust, you would not accept it. My sacrifice, O God, is a contrite spirit: a heart contrite and humbled, O God, you will not spurn." (Psalm 50:18-19) When people dedicate themselves to being contrite and humble as they interact with others, they soon discover the importance of other people's opinions and decisions. Such people grow in maturity, and thus become better people.
    Making sacrifices is one of the traditional ways of growing in spirituality in the Christian Church. We have been correctly taught that the more we have been able to

STAR TREK: FIRST CONTACT

give up personal preferences for the sake of the good of the whole, the better off we have been. The element of sacrifice is still a very important part of our spiritual growth. There are many situations in our school, at home, or with the community where we are asked to give up our own desires in order to help someone else. In this way, we develop a humble and contrite heart, and as a consequence become better people.

Preliminary Thought

21. What sacrifices are young people most often called to make?
22. What does it mean when you call a person "contrite and humble"?
23. It is one thing to give up a personal preference to help someone else. Is there anything worthwhile in other sacrifices, such as giving up candy for Lent and the like?

Notes

Reflection/Ideas/Discussion

WHAT SCENE DURING THIS SESSION STRIKES YOU THE MOST AND WHY?

24. Dialogue analysis: Cochran's statement: "Don't try to be a great man, just be a man." Why is this a good statement?
25. Dialogue analysis: The crew member's analysis of the Captain's decision: "Once the captain has made up his mind, the discussion is over." Is this good policy? Yes or no and why?

STAR TREK: FIRST CONTACT

26. Dialogue analysis: Lily argues with Picard about abandoning the Enterprise. Lily is probably right when she accuses Picard of showing vengeance. Can showing vengeance ever be morally correct? Yes or no and why?
27. Scene analysis: Picard apologizes to Worf. Why is asking forgiveness important for people?
28. Scene analysis: Picard decides to stay with the Enterprise as it self-destructs. Is it a good thing for the "captain to go down with the ship"? Yes or no and why?
29. Scene analysis: Picard offers himself in place of Data. It is the ultimate sacrifice for a person to lay down his life for a friend. In general, do you think that this type of giving exists in our world today? Yes or no and why?
30. Scene analysis: The aliens are Vulcans. Director Jonathan Frakes cleverly ties in this episode with other "Star Trek" series. Do you believe in extra-terrestrial life? Yes or no and why?
31. What lesson does the movie "Star Trek: First Contact" give to young people today?

Further Material

THE GREAT SANTINI

GENERAL THEME

A parent who has deep-seated mental problems will always influence the family in a negative way.

SESSION I
From: Begins right away.
To: After Ben says, "This little girl just whipped your ass good, Colonel," then slams the door of his room.
Approximate time: 37 minutes.

Theme: People with strong personalities often make it difficult on themselves and on others.

Scripture: **Mark 14:10-11** Judas betrays Jesus.

Doctrine/Application
[*Catechism of the Catholic Church* reference: number 1810-1811, 1822-1829]

There are many different personalities who walk the face of our earth. Some are happy and positive; some are unhappy and negative. Some are very open in their dealings with others; some remain very closed. And there are always some who are very weak, and likewise some who have what has been named "strong personalities." They are usually people who feel they have control of their lives, have very strong opinions about select topics, and who are not afraid to express those opinions among friends or even enemies.

Judas Iscariot may very well have been a person with a strong personality. We know from the Scriptures that he had expressed his opinion to Jesus concerning the poor. And we know he believed in his opinions enough to arrange for the capture of Jesus. (Mark 14:11) No doubt concluding that Jesus' thoughts and words were wrong and detrimental to the religious climate, he took the opportunity to follow his convictions. Judas with his strong personality, at the moment of talking to the chief priests, would never have considered his act a betrayal; it was to his mind, dedication to a principle.

Bull Meechum in the movie "The Great Santini" had strong principles, and he had a strong personality in which he would convey those principles. He was strong. He played strong; he believed strong; he lived strong; and he spoke strong. No wonder

THE GREAT SANTINI

that he found himself as a career Marine. The Marine mentality fit his personality to a tee. It was the means by which he conveyed his beliefs; it was the only way he could live his life. Consequently, he could see nothing wrong with the way he conducted that life. His was a vicious circle that saw a personality fit a way of life, and a way of life that kept feeding his beliefs. Finding no difficulty with his behavior, and therefore with no malice on his part at all, he began to hurt people, not the least of all, himself.

There are people of strong personalities, even early in life, as in high school and college. People who tend to dominate every conversation and every activity. Young people with strong personalities probably have many reasons for being the way they are, but there is no doubt that they should continually monitor both their motivation for being so strong, and what they do to other people.

Preliminary Thought

1. **As you study your high school or college, how would you describe the *most common* personality that you see? Use the categories of "weak, strong, happy, unhappy, positive and negative."**
2. **Give an example of someone who is totally convinced of her/his opinions, and is in fact, wrong.**
3. **The meditation calls attention to a "Marine mentality." In your opinion, what would a "Marine mentality" consist of? Why?**
4. **How do people with strong personalities in high school and college hurt themselves and others?**

Notes

THE GREAT SANTINI

Reflection/Ideas/Discussion

WHAT SCENE DURING THIS SESSION STRIKES YOU THE MOST AND WHY?

5. Analysis: What is your opinion of "the military" in your country? Do you think they carry out their objectives? Yes or no and why?
6. Scene analysis: The officers club. a) Do you believe that there is too much drinking of alcohol portrayed in movies? Yes or no and why? b) In general, do you think that there is too much drinking of alcohol among officers of the military? Yes or no and why?
7. Scene analysis: Meechum's children at attention as they listen to him. Obviously an exaggeration, the scene calls to mind very strict parents. Discuss how strict a parent should be, with regard to bed time, curfew, etc.
8. Dialogue analysis: Meechum's friend tells him that he never changes. Is it possible for a strong personality to change the way they behave?
9. Scene analysis: Meechum talks to his men. He portrays himself as a very mean person. Obviously, military people do not have to be "mean" in their approach to the people under them, but some are. In your opinion, why are they?
10. Scene analysis: Ben and Bull play basketball against each other. Bull is obviously angry that he lost. Why do we have such a strong stress in our country to win games?
11. Scene analysis: Bull keeps hitting Ben in the head with the basketball. Why was he doing it? Having seen the outcome as you did, what does the outcome "say" about the personalities of Ben and Bull?

Notes

THE GREAT SANTINI

SESSION II

From: After Ben says, "This little girl just whipped your ass good, Colonel," then slams the door of his room.

To: After the coach talks with Ben, telling him that he can't just forget about the incident.

Approximate time: 37 minutes.

Theme: We cannot live our lives vicariously through someone close to us.

Scripture: **Matthew 20:20-22** The mother of the sons of Zebedee makes a bold request.

Doctrine/Application

[*Catechism of the Catholic Church* **reference:** numbers 2221-2226.]

One of the most interesting phenomena to watch in our society is the way parents follow the growth of their children. It is all too obvious that parents must help their offspring attain the necessary goals to achieve adult maturity. When they do not, the lives of their children will almost always be impaired. Parents must be interested in what their children are doing: their academics, their extra-curricular activities, their social lives. But, when the parents' attention to their children's activities, is nothing more than a conduit for the parents to re-live their young years again, there is something wrong. The situation may be just as damaging to the young person as parents who neglect their children completely.

We do not know about the home life of the family we have come to know as Zebedee in the Gospels. All we know is that two sons of the family, James and John, were apostles of Jesus, and we know that in Matthew's Gospel, the mother of James and John made an unusually bold request. She could have been interested in the welfare of her sons, but she could also have been thinking about herself, and her own chance to share in Jesus' kingdom. If it were the latter, then there may have been serious difficulty with the Zebedee family.

There was serious difficulty with the Meechum family in the movie "The Great Santini." Bull Meechum, the loud, often obnoxious Marine father in the family, wanted his children to achieve. There was nothing wrong with that, but the intentions that guided such achievement were questionable. Bull Meechum lived his life again through his son Ben. He wanted Ben to be just like him because he thought he, the father and head of the family, was right, and therefore everything he wanted for himself, he felt his son should do. That included everything from drinking alcohol to playing basketball in high school. Bull Meechum was living his own life vicariously

THE GREAT SANTINI

through his son, dictating to him exactly the same philosophy that he had. As a consequence, his son Ben's life was stifled, and his maturity undermined.

Young people who find themselves with parents who are dominating their lives have a serious problem. Much like Ben Meechum, they may sense that the parent is wrong, but they still want to be part of the family. About the only thing that a young person can do in this instance is to have recourse to a counselor or a friend of the family who can give sound advice.

Preliminary Thought

12. In your opinion, what is the main problem with parents who are re-living their lives through their children?
13. Give an example of how parents live their own lives through their children.
14. If you know of someone whose family is being overly domineering toward him/her, what is the best thing that you could do?

Notes

Reflection/Ideas/Discussion

WHAT SCENE DURING THIS SESSION STRIKES YOU THE MOST AND WHY?

15. Scene analysis: Bull practices basketball at night in the rain. What does the action "say" about his character?
16. Dialogue analysis: Lillian Meechum says that harsh words were never fatal to anybody. True or false and why?

THE GREAT SANTINI

> 17. Scene analysis: Ben meets Toomer, and their relationship begins to blossom. [This is a very important part of the movie, and the instructor may want to develop the idea of prejudice, and the role prejudice plays in people's lives.] a) Why doesn't Ben show any prejudice toward Toomer? b) Why is prejudice so wrong?
> 18. Scene analysis: Ben reads the "birthday" letter from his mother. What is the principal difference between Bull and Lillian, his wife?
> 19. Scene analysis: Bull leads Ben into drinking and then getting drunk. What are the principal reasons why the action was wrong?
> 20. Scene analysis: Evidently Mary Ann Beechum feels rejected by her father because she is a girl. If a young person feels rejected by a parent, what is the best thing he/she can do?
> 21. Scene analysis: a) Bull tells Ben to retaliate toward the person who fouled him. Should Ben have disobeyed him? Yes or no and why? b) The coach seems to blame Ben for listening to his father. Was the coach correct? Yes or no and why?

Notes

SESSION III

From: After the coach talks with Ben, telling him that he can't just forget about the incident.
To: End.
Approximate time: 39 minutes.

Theme: Parents will always influence their children.

Scripture: **Ephesians 6:1-4** Paul gives his opinions concerning how a family should function together.

THE GREAT SANTINI

Doctrine/Application
[*Catechism of the Catholic Church* reference: numbers 2228-2231]

How much influence does a father have on a family? Most psychologists would answer that there is at least some influence, if not a major amount. In particular, how much influence does a verbally abusive father have on a family, especially if he has what we have called a "strong personality," that is, a very opinionated person who is not reticent about his opinions. Again, most psychologists would agree that most probably such a father has a significant amount of power that reaches well into the child's adult life. Some of the influence may be good, but by far most of it has the potential to be damaging to the psyche of the child.

The movie "The Great Santini" does not last long enough to be able to see the portrayal of Ben's and the other children's adult lives, but it is certain that their father had a significant effect on them as they grew up. In particular, Ben felt his father's presence and grew up both with his help and in spite of his help.

In Paul the Apostle's opinion, reiterating one of the ten commandments given to Moses, sons or daughters should honor their father and mother. But, Paul gives a special directive to the father, saying, "Fathers, do not provoke your children to anger, but bring them up with the training and instruction of the Lord." (Ephesians 6:4) As Paul views it, the fourth commandment works both ways.

Bull Meechum probably did not read Paul's letter to the Ephesians, or if he did, he did not pay any attention to it, since his children, and in particular, Ben, took the brunt of their father's anger and tirades. If some application were to be given to this reading from Scripture and the last session of the movie, most of it would be directed toward the parents. But if there is an application to the young people who have a father who is a tyrant, it could only be the recommendation that such young people seek the constant help of their mother or some other adult so that they could work out the problems that will almost assuredly come in the future. Older young people should also look carefully at their own idea of parenting and how they should act as a parent when they become one in a few short years.

Preliminary Thought

22. In your opinion, using as a measure a scale of 1-10 where 10 is high, how much bad influence does a "tyrant" father have on a son in the family? On a daughter? Why did you assign the number you did?

THE GREAT SANTINI

> 23. a) What is the most important thing a high school young person should give to his/her father and mother? Describe your answer in practical terms. b) What is the most important thing a father and mother should give to their children? Again, describe your answer.
> 24. In your opinion, describe the "discipline" that parents should use with their young children. With their older teenage children.

Notes

> ### Reflection/Ideas/Discussion
>
> **WHAT SCENE DURING THIS SESSION STRIKES YOU THE MOST AND WHY?**
>
> 25. Scene analysis: The Toomer incident. a) At the beginning of the confrontation, should Toomer have taken what he did without doing anything? What do you think Jesus would have done at this incident? b) Ben directly disobeys his father. When *should* a young person disobey a parent? c) Should we have as much "love" for animals as we do? Yes or no and why? d) Ben tells Bull that he did what Bull would have done. Why did Bull get so angry? e) Dialogue analysis: Ben to Bull—"Nobody tells you anything, Dad." Did the statement have any effect on Bull at all? Yes or no and why?
> 26. Scene analysis: The physical abuse on Lillian. Counselors advise wives who have been beaten by their husbands to leave the situation as soon as possible. Do you agree with this approach? Yes or no and why?

THE GREAT SANTINI

27. Scene analysis: Ben finds Bull in a depressed state. a) Why do you think Bull felt the way he did at that point? b) Why did Bull react the way he did when Ben told him that he loved him?
28. Scene analysis: Bull dies in the accident. After watching what he had done in his life, what was your first reaction?
29. Dialogue analysis: Lillian tells the children that they will not cry in public because their father would not like it. What is your feeling about this direction?
30. Dialogue analysis: Ben tells his mother that he used to pray that his father would die in an accident. What would be your response to Ben?
31. Scene analysis: Ben is leading the family as they leave the home, and the same thing happens as when Bull was in charge of moving. What do you think this says about the future of the Meechum family?

Further Material

THE GREAT SANTINI

THE LOST WORLD

GENERAL THEME

If human beings are governed only by what they want, they will have no respect for animal, man or God.

SESSION I
From: Begins right away.
To: After two of InGen's crew discover the small "scavenger" dinosaur and chase him away with an electrical shock, and one says, "Now, it does."
Approximate time: 40 minutes.

Theme: Evil desires often drive people more than good desires.

Scripture: **Luke 11:24-26** Jesus speaks of the high energy of unclean spirits.

Doctrine/Application
[*Catechism of the Catholic Church* **reference:** numbers 1706-1707]

One of the characteristics of evil is its persistence. Jesus attests to it as he talks of how evil works in the world. After the evil spirit finds someone who has resisted evil successfully, the evil spirit does not remain idle. But, "it goes and brings back seven other spirits more wicked than itself who move in and dwell there." (Luke 11:26) It is the same with the evil that dwells in the hearts of people. Perhaps because of the evil influence that surrounds us, evil desires often drive people more than good desires do. It seems a commonplace occurrence to witness people with evil desires work with incredible energy to accomplish their end, while people with good intentions simply do not have the same energy.

Witness the two groups in the movie "The Lost World" who want to know more about the phenomenal island where Jurassic-age dinosaurs have been developed. One group seems harmless enough to begin with, wanting to develop a photo-record of what has occurred. But, once the observation team sees how much money can be made with their pictures and photography, they easily forget about their photo-record. The other group from the very beginning are driven by greed and the pleasure of hunting the animals. For this group, there is no other consideration: they want as much as they can get out of the situation which has fallen into their hands. Both groups are moved by evil intentions, and seem to be willing to do as much as possible to accomplish their ends.

THE LOST WORLD

It is a cliché to say that evil knows no bounds. Once evil intentions have been given full reign and acceptance, it seems that the voice of good is a small cry amid the shouts of evil. Of course, we will not have the opportunity to work with a magical island as the groups in the movie, but we do have the opportunity to experience both good and evil intentions within ourselves and others. As we watch how evil tendencies seem to outshine the good tendencies in the movie, perhaps we should learn a lesson that is not an easy lesson to learn. Too often in our own personal world, we allow our own evil and the evil of others to dominate a situation while the good remains idle.

Preliminary Thought

1. a) On a universal level, in your opinion, what is the worst evil in the world today? b) On a local level, what is the worst evil around you?
2. Do you agree with the meditation that in general, it is a commonplace occurrence that people with evil intentions have more drive than people with good intentions? Yes or no and why?
3. Give an example where you have seen that people with evil intentions have more drive than people with good intentions.

Notes

Reflection/Ideas/Discussion

WHAT SCENE DURING THIS SESSION STRIKES YOU THE MOST AND WHY?
4. Scene analysis: The man on the subway makes fun of Dr. Malcolm. Why do people "make fun" of others?

THE LOST WORLD

5. Dialogue analysis: Hammond says that he won't make the same mistakes again, and as a matter of fact, he does make the same mistakes. What was the main reason why he made the same mistake?
6. Analysis: Malcolm's daughter is African American. a) What is your opinion about interracial marriages right now? b) Some churches discourage these marriages. Is there any reason for a church to forbid such marriages? Yes or no and why? c) Do you believe that there is any reason to forbid white couples from adopting babies of different countries? Yes or no and why?
7. Dialogue/scene analysis: Dr. Malcolm and his daughter argue. They both say words to one another that they should not have said. Given such an argument in a family, what is the ideal way to resolve the situation?
8. Dialogue analysis: Sarah says she is not afraid of the island, and that Malcolm is. a) Define fear. b) Do you think that you have to experience something before you can fear it? Yes or no and why?
9. Scene analysis: InGen comes on to the island and begins the process of hunting and trapping the dinosaurs. a) Do you think that this is cruelty to animals? Yes or no and why? b) What is your feeling about hunting deer, pheasants, and the like?

Notes

SESSION II

From: After two of InGen's crew discover the small "scavenger" dinosaur and chase him away with an electrical shock, and one says, "Now, it does."

To: While Sarah is in the tent, and hears the T-Rex coming, and says, "Oh no."

Approximate time: 41 minutes.

Theme: Good deeds often end up hurting the people who bring them about.

THE LOST WORLD

Scripture: **Acts 4:18-21** Peter and John risk their deaths in order the preach the word of God.

Doctrine/Application
[*Catechism of the Catholic Church* reference: numbers 2473-2474]

Good deeds often end up hurting the people who bring them about. But for the people who really care about others, there is no hesitation in doing them. They are convinced that the deeds should be done, and even if there is a threat of death, they believe that they should carry on with the deeds.

Such was the conviction of Peter and John as they spoke the words of God immediately after their leader Jesus died. As they explained to the people who could easily order their deaths, "It is impossible for us not to speak about what we have seen and heard." (Acts 4:20) They were so convinced that Jesus was the source of salvation for everyone in the world, that they felt compelled to deliver the message.

Although they are entirely different circumstances, we see two separate actions of real caring during this session of "The Lost World". Both actions portray real concern for others on the part of the people who are performing them. Nick and Sarah help a wounded infant dinosaur, and a little bit later, as a result of that action, Eddie Carr, a member of the their crew, decides to help his crew-mates no matter what the consequences.

Martyrdom was never the consideration of Peter and John as they preached about the salvation of humankind. Nor was it a thought for Nick and Sarah and Eddie as they struggled with the forces of nature and incredible animals in the movie "The Lost World." Martyrdom is hardly ever sought after, but it can be a consequence of people who are committed to a cause.

As Christians pursue their lives, there will be moments when they are so convinced that something is right that they risk their lives. Sometimes they may think about what the consequences of their conviction might be, while most of the time they will simply do what they believe is right, without thinking of what might happen. Whether or not they know what the end results might be, from the smallest act of charity for someone else, to the defense of the world as we know it, the true Christian will do the good. A good person who is out to do good things never figures the cost.

Preliminary Thought

10. Who are some people that you would consider truly committed to Jesus' way?
11. Who would you consider to be martyrs for the cause of Christianity today?

THE LOST WORLD

12. What are some good things that young people should do today which might have consequences that could be harmful?

Notes

Reflections/Ideas/Discussion

WHAT SCENE DURING THIS SESSION STRIKES YOU THE MOST AND WHY?

13. Scene analysis: Hammond's assistant releases the caged dinosaurs. In your mind, was there a better way of resolving the situation? Yes or no and why?
14. Scene analysis: Sarah and Nick care for the dinosaur. With her knowledge of animals, Sarah should not have done it, since she knew that the mother would come looking for the baby. Can you think of instances in modern life where people choose to care for something even though there will be severe consequences? Yes or no and why?
15. Scene analysis: As the trailer falls off the cliff, there are many heroics performed on behalf of each other. In real life, in general, do you think that people are willing to "give up their lives" on behalf of others? Yes or no and why?
16. Scene analysis: The InGen people help Sarah and the others to safety: that is, the "evil people" help the "good." The InGen people probably did not believe they were doing anything wrong by capturing or killing the animals. What course of action should a person follow if friends are doing something wrong and they don't realize it is wrong?
17. Scene analysis: The scavenger dinosaurs kill a man. As you view the violence that is shown here and elsewhere in the movie, do you think that movies that portray violence influence young people the wrong way? Yes or no and why?

THE LOST WORLD

Notes

SESSION III
From: While Sarah is in the tent, and hears the T-Rex coming, and says, "Oh no."
To: End.
Approximate time: 41 minutes.

Theme: We should have the utmost respect for nature, but our greed often does violence to it.

Scripture: **Genesis 1:28-31** God gave the earth and everything in it to human beings to care for and cultivate.

Doctrine/Application
[*Catechism of the Catholic Church* reference: numbers 2415-2418]

The Catechism of the Catholic Church, in its discussion of the seventh commandment, states that "The seventh commandment enjoins respect for the integrity of creation. Animals, like plants and inanimate beings, are by nature destined for the common good of past, present and future humanity. ... Man's dominion over inanimate and other living beings granted by the Creator (Genesis 1: 29-30) is not absolute; it is limited by concern for the quality of life of his neighbor, including generations to come; it requires a religious respect for the integrity of creation." (*Catechism,* number 2415)

The people who made up the institution known as InGen in the movie "The Lost World" were much too interested in their own desires than to be concerned with the "integrity of creation." When people become concerned only for what they want and what they can get out of life, they often will do violence to anything that stands in the way. Unfortunately, the American people have a history of doing just that, especially as we began to set up our country.

Perhaps one of the very best directives concerning how we should respect nature was given by a letter attributed to Chief Seattle, chief of the Duwamish, Suquamish and

THE LOST WORLD

allied Indian tribes, in 1854. The letter was sent to President Franklin Pierce. Its contents prove to be fruitful meditation for any student of nature and the human being. "Your destiny is a mystery to us," Chief Seattle writes. "What will happen when the buffalo are all slaughtered? The wild horses tamed? What will happen when the secret corners of the forest are heavy with the scent of many men and the view of the ripe hills is blotted by talking wires? Where will the thicket be? Gone! Where will the eagle be? Gone! And what is it to say goodbye to the swift pony and the hunt? The end of living and the beginning of survival." [The entire letter is placed in the **Preliminary Thought** and can afford profitable discussion.]

Preliminary Thought

18. The instructor might want to engage the students in discussion of the whole section from *The Catechism,* numbers 2415-2418.

19. The letter of Chief Seattle referred to in the meditation has many statements that could lead to fruitful discussion:

The President in Washington sends word that he wishes to buy our land. But how can you buy or sell the sky? The land? The idea is strange to us. If we do not own the freshness of the air and the sparkle of the water, how can you buy them?

Every part of this earth is sacred to my people. Every shining pine needle, every sandy shore, every mist in the dark woods, every meadow, every humming insect. All are holy in the memory and experience of my people.

We know the sap which courses through the trees as we know the blood that courses through our veins. We are part of the earth and it is part of us. The perfumed flowers are our sisters. The bear, the deer, the great eagle, these are our brothers. The rocky crests, the juices in the meadow, the body heat of the pony, and man, all belong to the same family.

The shining water that moves in the streams and rivers is not just water, but the blood of our ancestors. If we sell you our land, you must remember that it is sacred. Each ghostly reflection in the clear waters of the lakes tells of events and memories in the life of my people. The water's murmur is the voice of my father's father.

The rivers are our brothers. They quench our thirst. They carry our canoes and feed our children. So you must give to the rivers the kindness you would give any brother.

If we sell you our land, remember that the air is precious to us, that the air shares its spirit with all the life it supports. The wind also gives our children the spirit of life. So if we sell you our land, you must keep it apart and sacred, as a place where man can go to taste the wind that is sweetened by the meadow flowers.

Will you teach your children what we have taught our children? That the earth is our mother? What befalls all the sons of the earth.

This we know: the earth does not belong to man, man belongs to the earth. All things are connected like the blood that unites us all. Man did not weave the web of life, he is merely a strand in it. Whatever he does to the web, he does to himself.

THE LOST WORLD

> One thing we know: our god is also your god. The earth is precious to him and to harm the earth is to heap contempt on its creator.
>
> Your destiny is a mystery to us. What will happen when the buffalo are all slaughtered? The wild horses tamed? What will happen when the secret corners of the forest are heavy with the scent of many men and the view of the ripe hills is blotted by talking wires? Where will the thicket be? Gone! Where will the eagle be? Gone! And what is it to say goodbye to the swift pony and the hunt? The end of living and the beginning of survival.
>
> When the last Red Man has vanished with his wilderness and his memory is only the shadow of a cloud moving across the prairie, will these shores and forest still be here? Will there be any of the spirit of my people left?
>
> We love this earth as a newborn loves its mother's heartbeat. So, if we sell you our land, love it as we have loved it. Care for it as we have cared for it. Hold in your mind the memory of the land as it is when you receive it. Preserve the land for all children and love it, as God loves us all.
>
> As we are part of the land, you too are part of the land. This earth is precious to us. It is also precious to you. One thing we know: there is only one God. No man, be he Red Man or White Man, can be apart. We are brothers after all.

Notes

Reflection/Ideas/Discussion

WHAT SCENE DURING THIS SESSION STRIKES YOU THE MOST AND WHY?

20. Scene analysis: As the T-Rex chases people, people are crushed and killed, and the raptors begin killing people. People dying in movies is so commonplace that we often do not even think of it. a) What is the best way to prepare for death? b) Does a sudden death frighten you in any way? Yes or no and why?
21. Scene analysis: The raptors attack Sarah, Malcolm and Kelly. If you were close to the possibility of dying, how would you behave?

THE LOST WORLD

22. Scene analysis: The T-Rex comes into San Diego. This scene, perhaps more than any other place in the movie, shows what happens when human beings "mess around with nature." What is the worse thing we do to animals today?
23. Scene analysis: Ludlow goes into ship to take the infant dinosaur. His greed governs him to the end. Do people become so greedy that they even risk their lives to get what they want? Yes or no and why?
24. Scene analysis: Ludlow dies. Generally speaking, when evil people die, we feel no regrets. In real life, some states allow for capital punishment, namely, the legitimate killing of people. What is your opinion about capital punishment, and why do you feel that way. [See *Catechism of the Catholic Church*, number 2266, but see later editions for further commentary.]
25. Dialogue analysis: Dr. Hammond's interview on CNN. During the interview, he says it is imperative that we establish rules for the preservation and isolation of the island, that the creatures require the absence of human beings for survival, and that if we can step aside, life will find a way. Comment on his interview.
26. What is the most important lesson of the movie "The Lost World"?

Further Material

THE LOST WORLD

THE MAN WITHOUT A FACE

GENERAL THEME

The gift of trust and love is the greatest gift a friend can give another.

SESSION I
From: Begins right away.
To: After Megan says, "Let me come with you, please, come on, Chuck," and Chuck looks at her.
Approximate time: 36 minutes.

Theme: We cannot live by ourselves all our lives; we need other people.

Scripture: **Genesis 2:18-24** God recognizes that it is not good for man to be alone.

Doctrine/Application
[*Catechism of the Catholic Church* **reference:** number 2196]
From the very beginning of creation, it was evident that one of the problems that humankind would have to face would be the problem of loneliness. So the Lord God says, "It is not good for the man to be alone." (Genesis 2:18) Anticipating the human nature of man and woman, the Lord God could see what we human beings have a tendency to do. We can be so concerned about ourselves and become so wrapped up in our own problems, that we often forget about others, sometimes, deliberately. Simon and Garfunkel's classic song "I Am A Rock" can actually be a biography of some human beings.

A winter's day in a deep and dark December,
I am alone,
gazing from my window to the streets below
on a freshly fallen silent shroud of snow;
I am a rock, I am an island.
I build walls,
a fortress deep and mighty, than none may penetrate.
I have no need of friendship;
friendship causes pain:
it's laughter and it's loving I disdain.

THE MAN WITHOUT A FACE

I am a rock, I am an island.
Don't talk of love;
Well, I've heard the word before.
It's sleeping in my memory.
I won't disturb this slumber of feelings that have died.
If I'd never loved, I never would have cried.
I am a rock, I am an island.
I have my books and my poetry to protect me;
I am shielded in my armor, hiding in my room,
safe within my womb;
I touch no one, and no one touches me.
I am a rock, I am an island.

Justin McLeod was such a man. He wanted no one to bother him on his island away from touch and love. Often angry at what the world had done to him and his life, he could not see beyond the physical and psychological scars that were part of his life. Then a young boy became curious, and Justin McLeod changed. Beginning to see how it was necessary even for him to have a friend, he discovered that he could still love.

Unfortunately, there is not a lack of opportunities for human beings to be hurt because of others or because things do not go right for them in life. There are many reasons to feel bitter and angry and upset. It is at such times that we want to become the rocks and the islands that no one can approach. We do it to make ourselves feel better, to help cover over some of the pain and to protect ourselves from getting hurt again.. But, the Lord God's words continue to ring true for all: "It is not good for man to be alone." We must have the help of others, even as we desire something else.

Preliminary Thought

1. **Do you think that there is ever a good reason to completely shut ourselves off from others? Yes or no and why?**
2. **The phrase from Simon and Garfunkel's song: "If I'd never loved, I never would have cried." Is it true or false and why?**
3. **If you have a friend who is lonely, what is the best way to help him/her?**

Notes

THE MAN WITHOUT A FACE

> Reflection/Ideas/Discussion
>
> **WHAT SCENE DURING THIS SESSION STRIKES YOU THE MOST AND WHY?**
>
> 4. Scene analysis: As Charles was dreaming in the opening scene, he spoke of the "Hugh Hefner philosophy of life." Hugh Hefner, the creator of the magazine "Playboy", in many ways, symbolizes an empire built on sex. What do you think the "Hugh Hefner philosophy of life" means?
> 5. Scene analysis: The children fight in the car. What is the principal reason that brothers and sisters fight, sometimes bitterly?
> 6. Dialogue analysis: The children realize that "marriage" is their mother's hobby. When a mother chooses many mates, what effect does it have on the children?
> 7. Scene analysis: Charles vandalizes the vehicles. a) Why did Charles do it? b) What is the reason why young people vandalize?
> 8. Scene analysis: Charles does not understand how McLeod is teaching him. What do you think are the most important characteristics of a teacher?
> 9. Dialogue analysis: The people of the town talk about McLeod. Why do people talk about others when they really know nothing about them?
> 10. Dialogue analysis: Charles says he hates writing. Why is writing so necessary for life?

Notes

THE MAN WITHOUT A FACE

SESSION II

From: After Megan says, "Let me come with you, please, come on, Chuck," and Chuck looks at her.

To: After Charles leaves and McLeod anxiously begins to look at Charles' test.

Approximate time: 36 minutes.

Theme: True friendship involves the true sharing of ideals and ideas.

Scripture: **John 7:45-52** Nicodemus speaks in favor of Jesus.

Doctrine/Application
[*Catechism of the Catholic Church* reference: number 2347]

Scripture does not tell us much about the Pharisee named Nicodemus. We know that he came to Jesus secretly and we know he spoke in favor of him on one occasion. At that time, at the risk of being ridiculed by his fellow Pharisees, Nicodemus defended Jesus: "Does our law condemn a person before it first hears him and finds out what he is doing?" (John 7:51) Reading in between the lines, we might conclude that Nicodemus had built up a friendship with Jesus, a friendship that had led to a discovery of what Jesus was all about and what his ideals and ideas were.

As friendships develop in our lives, much of what makes us friends are ideas and ideals that we share, even when we do not always completely agree. Justin McLeod and Charles Norstadt spend time with each other during this session of "A Man Without A Face." McLeod was Charles' mentor; he was much more older and mature, but both he and Charles were in need of a friend. Gradually, they began to share their own ideas and ideals, and because of it, the friendship grew between the two.

We all develop friendships as we grow. Many of those friendships will last a long time, many will not. Studying Justin McLeod's and Charles Norstadt's unlikely friendship should lead us to see the value of risking the sharing of ourselves with each other as we work on a friendship. Friends who are willing to take such a risk have a foundation which can last a lifetime.

Preliminary Thought

11. Realizing Nicodemus' involvement with Jesus (see also John 3:1 ff together with the passage of this session), what conclusions, if any, can be made about Nicodemus' character.

THE MAN WITHOUT A FACE

12. In general, do you think that close friendships between someone as old as Justin McLeod and as young as Charles Norstadt are common? Yes or no and why?
13. In general, do most friendships between young people share some deeper ideas and ideals? Yes or no and why?

Notes

Reflection/Ideas/Discussion

WHAT SCENE DURING THIS SESSION STRIKES YOU THE MOST AND WHY?

14. Dialogue analysis: Charles calls McLeod "pukehead." Why do many young people use shocking language?
15. Scene analysis: Charles stares at McLeod's scars. Do you think that McLeod is "too touchy" about his condition? Yes or no and why?
16. Dialogue analysis: Charles tells McLeod that he hates poetry. Why do you think students should study poetry?
17. Dialogue analysis: "People are afraid of what they don't know." Give an example which proves this statement.
18. Dialogue analysis: "Take some responsibility for what you want." What does McLeod mean with this statement?
19. Dialogue/scene analysis: Charles lies about telling his mother. Why do you think he didn't want to tell his mother?
20. Scene analysis: Shakespeare "comes alive" for Charles as he and McLeod act it out. Why is the study of Shakespeare important for a young person?

THE MAN WITHOUT A FACE

> 21. Dialogue/scene analysis: Charles asks McLeod about sex and the attraction of man for woman. a) When should "sex education" be given to a young person? b) Do you think that public schools should give "sex education" courses? Yes or no and why?
> 22. Scene analysis: Charles' young friends are smoking as they are relaxing. a) Why do young people smoke cigarettes? b) What can be done to get them to cease?
> 23. Scene analysis: Charles dreams about what happens after he told of McLeod's accident. What do you think director Mel Gibson is "saying" with this scene?
> 24. Scene analysis: The dad offers a beer to the young boys. Do you believe that this action is good or bad for the young people? Explain your answer.
> 25. Dialogue/scene analysis: McLeod encourages Charles to tell him why he is acting so strangely, and Charles tells him. Because both McLeod and Charles trust each other, they are able to be open with each other. In general, do you think that young people's close relationships achieve this openness with each other? Yes or no and why?

Notes

SESSION III

From: After Charles leaves and McLeod anxiously begins to look at Charles' test.
To: End.
Approximate time: 36 minutes.

Theme: In a true friendship, there can be no room for selfishness.

Scripture: **1 Samuel 20:41-42** David and Jonathan's friendship.

THE MAN WITHOUT A FACE

Doctrine/Application
[*Catechism of the Catholic Church* **reference:** number 2342, 2346, 2347]

During this final session of "A Man Without A Face," director Mel Gibson puts the character he plays, Justin McLeod, into a situation involving a choice. He can either protect himself and possibly hurt his new young friend Charles Norstadt or he can run away from the problem, thus admitting guilt where there was none. He made his choice based on friendship rather than selfishness.

One of the proven signs of friendship is when the concern we have for a friend becomes more important than our own desires. Too many so-called friends enjoy the friendship from their point of view only. When a crisis occurs in which someone may look bad or could get hurt, people often choose themselves over their friends.

As we study Jonathan's concern for his friend David in the Hebrew Scriptures first book of Samuel, it becomes very clear that his is a real friendship. Time and time again with no regard for his own fear from his father, Jonathan proved to be a friend to David. (1 Samuel 20:41-42)

Both Jonathan of the Hebrew Scriptures and Justin McLeod of "A Man Without A Face" teach a valuable lesson about friendship. In a friendship which can be regarded as true, there is no place for selfishness.

Preliminary Thought

26. Define selfishness, especially with regard to friendship.
27. The meditation makes the point that *concern* for a friend is a sign of friendship. What are some other signs of true friendship?
28. The movie will end with a magnificent statement from McLeod to Norstadt which suggests the importance of the truth and knowing the truth. In general, do you think most young people have a true respect for the truth? Yes or no and why?

Notes

THE MAN WITHOUT A FACE

Reflection/Ideas/ Discussion

WHAT SCENE DURING THIS SESSION STRIKES YOU THE MOST AND WHY?

29. Scene analysis: McLeod "rewards" Charles for his hard work with the test, and arranges a ride in the sea-plane. Recognizing that McLeod has become a father-figure for Norstadt, in general, a) Do most fathers show this type of concern for their sons? Yes or no and why? b) Specifically, what is the role of a father as a young boy grows?

30. Dialogue analysis: Charles to McLeod: "I can't see your scars anymore." What is the significance of this statement?

31. Scene analysis: In anger, Gloria tells Charles about his real father. Granted, Gloria was angry, but do you think young people have an understanding of "confidentiality," that is, that some things must be kept secret at all times? Yes or no and why?

32. Scene analysis: McLeod holds Norstadt as he cries. Psychiatrists specializing in children always advise a close male bond between father and son. In your opinion, do most fathers show this affection to their sons? Yes or no and why?

33. Scene analysis: With Norstadt only wearing underwear, the thought of everyone connected with the scene is that there was some sort of sexual misconduct on the part of McLeod. Why do people "automatically" think this way?

34. Scene analysis: The police want to meet with McLeod. They said it was to get the facts. What was their real intention? Why did they feel the way they did, and was it justified or not?

35. Scene analysis: Gloria and Charles "make up" in a sense. Sibling rivalry has always been a problem for children as they grow. What is the best advice that you can think of concerning discipline to give to parents who have young children?

36. Dialogue analysis: Charles asks McLeod whether he ever abused the boy who was killed in the car accident. McLeod does not answer directly, but calls for his trust. Why is it often so difficult to trust others?

THE MAN WITHOUT A FACE

37. Scene analysis: McLeod meets with the "board," and accuses them of being interested only in the "appearance" of the truth. a) Do you agree with him? Yes or no and why? b) Quite obviously, McLeod backs down from making the truth clear when he finds that it could hurt Charles. This is the lesson of this session. It is comparable to "martyrdom" on McLeod's part since he would have to alter his entire life. Would most people be willing to make that kind of sacrifice for a friend? Yes or no and why?
38. Dialogue analysis: McLeod's letter to Charles: "Hello, Norstadt. I'm sorry, but I'm not allowed to see you. I'm not allowed to talk to you. I'm not allowed to write you this letter. These are my concessions and their conditions. Or what I hope any good teacher would call a lesson in the tender mercies of injustice. But strangely, this is nothing to grieve over. Because you know the truth and I now know that you can outgrow a part, even a sad one. You taught me that. You gave me what I never expected to find again: a gift of your trust and love. And nothing can take that grace away. The best is yet to be, Norstadt, so do it well. I remain as ever your tutor, Justin McLeod." What strikes you most about the letter and why?
39. Final scene. What did you feel as you watched it? Charles' words: "But there's a face before me now, somewhere out beyond the edge of the crowd." It gave him hope to have "everything perfect."
40. What is the most important lesson that a young person can learn from the movie "A Man Without A Face"?

Further Material

THE MAN WITHOUT A FACE

THE SPITFIRE GRILL

GENERAL THEME

In order to know people completely, we have to comprehend why they act the way they do.

SESSION I
From: Begins right away.
To: After Percy leaves with Hannah's list and money, and Hannah addresses her dog with the words, "What do you think?"
Approximate time: 38 minutes.

Theme: Gossip is one of the great evils among people.

Scripture: **James 3:2b-10** The power of the human tongue.

Doctrine/Application
[*Catechism of the Catholic Church* **reference:** numbers 2477-2479]

Moral theologians dispute when a mortal sin is committed, even *if* there is such a thing as a mortal sin anymore. But if there is an area where high school and college age people can commit a mortal sin, it is in the area of speech. Young people talk about other people. It is one of the primary topics of conversation. Discovering for the first time how people talk, think and act, teenagers will necessarily want to discuss what other people are doing and why they are doing it. It is the teenager's pastime.

What makes such a pastime morally wrong is the manner in which young people speak of others. Many times it turns into rumor-laden gossip, with innuendo and exaggeration which tend to make a great story, but often do not match the truth. The Christian letter of James addresses such a topic, calling attention to the way everyone of us uses our tongue. "If anyone does not fall short in speech," James writes, "he is a perfect man, able to bridle his whole body also." Unfortunately, there are many who fall short in many respects. "The tongue," he bluntly says, "is ... a fire. It exists among our members as a world of malice, defiling the whole body and setting the entire course of our lives on fire. ... With it we bless the Lord ... and with it we curse human beings who are made in the likeness of God." (James 3:2, 6, 9) Whether the sin of gossip is a mortal sin may be debatable, but there can be no debate that it is a sin.

THE SPITFIRE GRILL

Percy Talbot in the movie "The Spitfire Grill" has a background tailor-made for gossip, and the town of Gilead, Maine is just small enough for everyone to enjoy the possibility of a good story. As we observe the townspeople talking about Percy, and recognize exactly what it does to her, we must question ourselves.

How do we talk of people we do not know? How do we talk of others when we do not know all the facts? How do we speak of our "enemies," those who do not like us? Is it not true that we often want something to talk about even if we have to make up a few things to make it more interesting? People's reputations can be irreparably ruined by other people who speak without the proper knowledge. Gossip is an evil that is a sin. Young people must know its consequences as they grow.

> **Preliminary Thought**
>
> 1. [The instructor might want to prepare for this question. See *Catechism of the Catholic Church, nos. 1854-1864*.] a) How do you understand the meaning of a "mortal sin"? b) With such an understanding, do you think that there are many mortal sins committed? Yes or no and why?
> 2. Define "gossip" as you understand it.
> 3. In what areas do you find that most young people give into gossip?
> 4. Once gossip has ruined a reputation, what are the ways a person can gain a good reputation again?
> 5. On a scale of 1-10 where 10 is high, where do you rate the "problem of gossip" in your high school or college?

Notes

THE SPITFIRE GRILL

Reflection/Ideas/Discussion

WHAT SCENE DURING THIS SESSION STRIKES YOU THE MOST AND WHY?

6. Scene analysis: The movie begins in a prison. a) Do you believe that our prison system is a good one? Yes or no and why? b) Many people say that our prisons simply make criminals worse than they already are. Do you agree or disagree and why?
7. Scene analysis: Hannah gives Percy a place to live and work. In general, do you think people will give "strangers" this type of help as they begin their life over again? Yes or no and why?
8. Dialogue analysis: Percy yells out that she had been in prison. Why do you think she did this? Did it do any good at all?
9. Scene analysis: Joe and Percy go to the bar together. Percy evidently feels that Joe wants to be with her simply to find out about her past life. Do you think that Joe invited her for that reason? Yes or no and why?
10. Character analysis: Hannah Ferguson. From what you have seen in the first session of the movie, what type of person do you think she is? Why?
11. Scene analysis: Shelby comes and helps Percy. In general, do you believe that people try to help people when they are not asked first? Yes or no and why?
12. Dialogue analysis: Percy tries to talk to the man who takes the sack. Percy is obviously trying to reach out to him. Why do you think Percy is doing it?
13. Dialogue/scene analysis: Shelby tells Percy about Hannah's early life and why she wants to sell the restaurant. Her son Eli was obviously hurt seriously in some way in Vietnam. Discuss your feelings about the Vietnam conflict. a) From what you have studied about it, should America have been involved? Yes or no and why? b) Why do you think that the American people did not treat the Vietnam veterans with the respect they deserved when they came back?
14. Scene analysis: Hannah trusts Percy with the money. a) In general, do you believe that young people trust each other? Yes or no and why? b) In general, do they trust adults? Yes or no and why?

THE SPITFIRE GRILL

Notes

SESSION II

From: After Percy leaves with Hannah's list and money, and Hannah addresses her dog with the words, "What do you think?"

To: As Joe and Percy are talking in the woods, and Joe says, "I think maybe it could be real good news for us too."

Approximate time: 37 minutes.

Theme: Care and concern for another human person is one of the marks of love.

Scripture: **John 10:11-15** Jesus cares for his sheep.

Doctrine/Application
[*Catechism of the Catholic Church* **reference:** numbers 1822-1827]

Around Jerusalem where Jesus was speaking, there were many plains, abandoned and uncultured tracts of land which were good for nothing except pasturing sheep. Therefore Jesus' audience knew about shepherds and sheep.

Shepherds in particular were interesting people. Since Jesus compared himself to one, we have become accustomed to consider them to be gentle, understanding, and kind people. Actually as we have begun to discover more about Jesus' times, most shepherds were just the opposite. They were dirty, smelly, and ignorant individuals who did not respect the rules of religion; in fact, most of them did not appreciate religion at all. Some of them were thieves, most of them were tough characters who were not afraid to use their shepherd staffs as weapons.

Why then did Jesus compare himself to a shepherd? No one knows, of course, but much of the reason may lie in Jesus' understanding of the virtue of sincerity. The master who owned the sheep could depend on *good* shepherds. Unconcerned with show or what other people thought, good shepherds were sincere people.

THE SPITFIRE GRILL

Consequently, for Jesus, when he thought of himself as a good shepherd, he was probably thinking of the shepherds' sincere concern for their sheep.

As one studies the person of Percy Talbot in "The Spitfire Grill," one cannot help but think of sincerity. Like Jesus the good shepherd, Percy was concerned about the people around her. She wanted to help Hannah; she was very interested in the mysterious man who took the food from Hannah's yard; and she grew to be friends with Shelby. Percy Talbot was a sincere person who came to see the importance of love among her friends.

What about the sincerity in our lives? Because we are Christian, we are called to love, to really be concerned about, be willing to die for those with whom we work--our families, the people in our place of employment, the people that we run into every day. As we strive to be sincere in our approach to others, we know that we often take them for granted or judge them. If we are to be like a good shepherd, we will be people who really care about those around us.

Preliminary Thought

15. Define "sincerity" as you understand it.
16. The meditation concentrates on the "people that we run into every day." What are the best ways to show true love to those who are around us all the time?
17. In general, do you think that people tend to "judge" or "pre-judge" other people more than they should?

Notes

THE SPITFIRE GRILL

Reflection/Ideas/Discussion

18. Scene analysis: Shelby and Percy write the advertisement for "The Spitfire Grill." Develop an advertisement which concentrates on the good things for: a) your school, b) your family, c) your community.
19. Scene analysis: Percy makes the mysterious man something special for his sack and also includes some of her favorite pictures. Giving on behalf of others is an important part of love. a) In general, do you believe that Americans "give enough of themselves"? b) Do you think that most young people are generous to each other?
20. Dialogue/scene analysis: Shelby tells Percy about "church" and takes her there. a) Do you think people attend church as much as they should in today's age? Yes or no and why? b) Do you think young people attend church the way they should? Yes or no and why? c) What are the principal excuses that young people use to keep them away from church? d) Do you think any of the excuses mentioned are valid reasons to stay away from church? e) If you were designing a church service, what would it consist of?
21. Scene analysis: Percy visits Joe's father. Presuming that there was nothing the matter with him physically, why do adults behave as he did?
22. Scene analysis: Percy is hurt when Shelby talks of children, and later on at the waterfall. It will become obvious why she is hurt later on. What is the best way to work with the pain when someone else hurts our feelings?
23. Scene analysis: Percy "talks" to the mysterious man in the woods. Why do you think she is so interested in talking to him?
24. Scene analysis: Hannah allows Percy to rub her legs for her. What are the best ways that younger people can help older people?
25. Scene analysis: Everyone is happy. Overjoyed at all the money and essays which they have received, the whole town seems happy and contented. What are the essential characteristics of "being happy" with life?
26. Scene analysis: Hannah, Shelby and Percy laugh with each other. George Santayana (1863-1952), U. S. philosopher and poet wrote in *Dialogues in Limbo* that "The young man who has not wept is a savage, and the old man who will not laugh is a fool." Discuss what this means to you.
27. Dialogue/scene analysis: Nahum tells Shelby that she is not smart enough to have come up with the idea of the essay contest. How *should* have Shelby reacted to such a statement?

THE SPITFIRE GRILL

> 28. Dialogue analysis: As Percy massages Hannah's leg, Hannah says not to press too hard, and then speaks of the deep hurts that cause the pain. a) In your opinion, what is the cause of most pain for a young person today? b) What is the cause of most pain for an adult?
> 29. Dialogue analysis: Nahum is very concerned about Percy who has orchestrated the $200,000. Do you think his was a legitimate concern? Yes or no and why?
> 30. Scene analysis: The town meeting concerning the essays and selling of "The Spitfire Grill." What was the main concern of the townspeople, and was it a legitimate concern? Yes or no and why?

Notes

SESSION III

From: As Joe and Percy are talking in the woods, and Joe says, "I think maybe it could be real good news for us too."

To: End.

Approximate time: 37 minutes.

Theme: Before we make decisions concerning a person, we must know that person well.

Scripture: **Acts 9:10-17** The Lord teaches Ananias to know Paul the Apostle.

Doctrine/Application
[*Catechism of the Catholic Church* reference: number 2477]

In a surprising speech at the end of the movie "The Spitfire Grill," one of the people of Gilead, Percy's adopted home town, admits a lack of knowledge about Percy Talbot. It is surprising not only because of the person who speaks it, but also because it is even said. Most people will not own up to pre-judgment. We have a tendency to simply allow our thoughts concerning someone else to lead us where they may, and often they lead to conclusions that are far from the truth. Percy Talbot was the type of person that was perfect for pre-judgments. Her background was questionable, she was not a local person, and she did things that seemed different from what other people did. People easily guessed that they knew Percy Talbot, but the truth was that they did not.

An interesting character in the conversion of Paul the Apostle is the person who opened him to the Christian path. The Acts of the Apostles names him Ananias. Ananias thought he knew Paul the Apostle. After all, Paul was the ex-Pharisee that was persecuting the followers of the Way. Ananias knew what he thought and why he thought it, didn't he? So, he told the Lord, "I have heard from many sources about this man." (Acts 9:13) Ananias' problem was a simple one: he had failed to learn all the facts before he made his judgment.

Everyone of us makes judgments. We cannot function without doing it. Sometimes, the judgments must be made without all the facts. The lesson of this session of "The Spitfire Grill" likewise, the lesson of Paul's conversion, is that once we have made those judgments, we must allow ourselves some time. During the time, it is only right that we open ourselves to as much of the truth as possible, giving ourselves the opportunity to really know a situation or a person before proceeding further with decisions. It is a lesson that will enhance our lives.

Preliminary Thought

31. Do you agree with the meditation that "most people will not own up to pre-judgment"? Yes or no and why?
32. Name some situations in your life where you thought you knew the truth about something, and you discovered later that you were wrong in your judgment.
33. The meditation suggests that we give ourselves time before we act on judgments that we have made. Do you believe that most people practice this? Yes or no and why?

Notes

THE SPITFIRE GRILL

Reflection/Ideas/Discussion

34. Scene analysis: Percy tells Joe that she cannot have children. a) How important are children to a marriage? Why? b) If the couple wants to have children, how long after marriage should the couple wait in your opinion? Why? c) In your opinion, how many children should a couple have in today's world?

35. Scene analysis: Percy sees the ornament on her window sill. What is its significance for the movie?

36. Dialogue analysis: Percy sings as she walks in the field and then rests. She sings of a balm in Gilead which can make the world be whole and heal a worried soul. Obviously, Percy is "reaching" out to the mysterious man whom she calls "Johnny B." What are the characteristics of a person who truly cares for another?

37. Scene analysis: Hannah is very angry at Percy because Hannah thought Percy chased her son away. "I lost my son," she screams at Percy. One can easily see why she is so upset. This might be called "justifiable anger." When is anger justified?

38. Scene analysis: Nahum takes the money from the safe and places it in the sack in order to prevent Percy from "stealing" it, the same sack which later Percy gives to Eli. If Nahum felt the way he did about Percy, was there a better way he could have handled his concern?

39. Dialogue/scene analysis: Shelby tells Nahum that if he condemns her without proof, she will leave the marriage. Is that a good enough reason to end a marriage? Yes or no and why?

40. Dialogue/scene analysis: Percy tells Shelby about the "manslaughter" charge. a) Most theologians agree that murder is "permitted" when self-defense is involved. Do you agree and why or why not? b) Specifically in Percy's story, do you believe it was "self-defense"? Yes or no and why?

41. Scene analysis: Percy yells at Eli to run, trying to protect him. Was there any other way she could have handled the situation? Yes or no and why?

42. Scene analysis: Percy drowns while trying to help someone else. In general, do you feel that most Christian people have such a strong love that they will give their lives for someone else? Yes or no and why?

43. Scene analysis: During Percy's funeral, Joe stood, but did not say anything. In your opinion, explain why.

THE SPITFIRE GRILL

44. Dialogue analysis: Nahum's speech, and his statement that he thought he knew Percy Talbot, the source of the meditation for this session of the movie. In your opinion, when do you think you really *know* someone else?
45. Dialogue analysis: In Nahum's speech, he said that he was responsible for her death. He was and he wasn't. Given his feeling, however, what is the best way to overcome the pain he feels?
46. Scene analysis: Hannah and her son Eli. It can best be described as a "beautiful scene." What do you believe was going through Hannah's and Eli's minds?
47. Dialogue analysis: Clare's words of explanation concerning why she entered the contest: hoping that your town could be the place that gives her son a chance. a) What was the most important lesson the people of Gilead learned from the "Percy Talbot incident"? b) In general, what lesson should young people learn from it?

Further Material

VOLCANO

GENERAL THEME

In life, there will be tragedy, and we must learn to work with it, always keeping the importance of people in mind.

SESSION I

From: Begins right away.
To: After Emmit says to Mike: "Looking all over for her, Mike; nobody knows where she is."
Approximate time: 33 minutes.

Theme: People do not read signs of impending danger very well.

Scripture: **Matthew 16:1-4** Jesus tells his enemies to read the signs of the times.

Doctrine/Application
[*Catechism of the Catholic Church* **reference:** number 1430-1433]

It is axiomatic that with the possibility of hindsight, our vision of history would be so much clearer. We know, for example, that if we would have been just a little more aware, the history of humankind would have changed several times. The Ancient Roman Empire may not have disintegrated. The American Civil War may not have even started, let alone been settled the way it was. In the modern era, Americans may never have fought the Vietnam war. Many historical events of impending danger were actually clearly seen by someone somewhere because they could read the signs of what was happening. The problem was that people could not read the signs.

In fact, many people throughout the ages have had problems with reading signs of what was coming. Jesus referred to it in his lifetime when his enemies wanted him to do some magical signs. He points out to them that they should read some real signs, signs like Jonah the prophet who called for repentance. He is telling them to read the signs and know the consequences. (Matthew 16:1-4)

As we watch the beginning session of "Volcano," there are signs of immediate danger which are clearly noticed. But because people will complain about the loss of convenience or time, decisions are made with no respect for a possible impending catastrophe.

We will probably not have the opportunity to read signs which have to do with major events in the lives of the people of our world, but we should be able to read the

VOLCANO

signs of what is going on in our own small worlds. We often see signs that indicate that we are not doing some things correctly, like failing grades, or loss of friendships. One of the marks of personal maturity is to read the signs of possible danger in our lives, and be able to adjust accordingly. If we do, we may be able to prevent a tragedy in our own lives.

Preliminary Thought

1. As you consider your own past right now, what would you do differently if you would have known then what you know now?
2. As you consider our country, what are some signs that you can see which indicate that we should change the way we do things?
3. As you consider the lives of young people in particular, discuss some signs that young people should read, and then change their behaviors.

Notes

Reflections/Ideas/Discussion

WHAT SCENE DURING THIS SESSION STRIKES YOU THE MOST AND WHY?

4. Scene analysis: The drive-by shooting in Los Angeles. What are the major causes of unrest in our large cities?
5. Scene analysis: The earthquake. What is the best way to prepare for the possibility of a major earthquake?
6. Analysis: Kelly, a "typical" teenager. Do you think that most fourteen year olds behave the way Kelly did toward her dad and "baby-sitter"? Yes or no and why?

VOLCANO

> 7. Scene analysis: The construction workers betting on the center of the earthquake, and its level. What does this scene "say" to you about the seriousness with which Los Angeles people take earthquakes? Discuss your answer.
> 8. Dialogue analysis: Mike's "baby-sitter" for Kelly speaks of how Kelly behaved after Mike's divorce. In general, what does divorce do to the children of the marriage which has broken up?
> 9. Scene analysis: Stan refuses to stop the metro. If you were in his shoes, with only the knowledge which he had at that time, would you have done the same? Yes or no and why?
> 10. Dialogue analysis: Amy says that "certainty" is a big word for a scientist. In general, can a scientist really believe in God? Yes or no and why?
> 11. Scene analysis: Rachel, the scientist is killed by the lava, and you are led to believe that there are many who are killed later by the lava. Movies such as "Volcano" present the deaths of many people, often by violence. Do you think that we have lost the proper understanding of "death" in our world?
> 12. Scene analysis: Kelly says to her dad that they are going to die. Have you ever felt fear for your life before? If you have, describe the experience.
> 13. Analysis: If you knew that there was a very good possibility of death in the next hour, what would you do?

Notes

SESSION II

From: After Emmit says to Mike: "Looking all over for her, Mike; nobody knows where she is."

To: After the men are moving the barricade, and Mike says, "Move over there." (Before the scene at the hospital.)

Approximate time: 35 minutes.

VOLCANO

Theme: In times of stress, people must act in a mature manner.

Scripture: **Matthew 2:13-15**   Joseph acts maturely in very difficult circumstances.

Doctrine/Application
[*Catechism of the Catholic Church* **reference:** numbers 1781-1782]

There can be little doubt that Joseph, the foster father of Jesus, knew about stress in his young life. As we pursue the story of the circumstances surrounding Jesus' birth in Matthew's Gospel, Joseph had already taken Mary into his home against his original inclination. He had to travel with her to Bethlehem. The trip was difficult enough and even more difficult since his wife was pregnant. Now, at the direction of an angel, he had to take his wife and new child to Egypt, again no easy journey. But, that which proved to be the most stressful no doubt, was the fact that people were trying to destroy the child. In the midst of all the stress, Joseph behaved in a mature manner, accepting the dangers as opportunities to serve his family better. (Matthew 2:13-15)

A catastrophe in progress is incredibly stressful. The people of Los Angeles felt the pressure of panic all around them. In particular, the people connected with the Office of Emergency Management, the people who were in charge during such a disturbance, were under unbelievable stress. During this session of "Volcano," such stress is portrayed especially with Kelly and Mike, daughter and father, while Mike works as Director of the Office of Emergency Management. We also see it among the workers who were involved in preventing the lava flow, and in particular between a white policeman and black citizen who felt that his rights were being violated because of his color.

There are times of stress in our lives, not to the extent of the movie "Volcano," but times of stress nonetheless. Things do not go right for us, we have too many things to be done, we have a major exam or presentation on which our future depends—times of stress. During those times, it is imperative that we maintain our composure. It might mean talking to someone who can help us or turning to God in prayer, but it will always mean approaching the crisis with maturity.

Preliminary Thought

14. **What are the principal elements of stress in a young person's life today?**
15. **What do you believe are the most stressful jobs in our country at the present time? Why?**
16. **What are the usual ways that a young person handles stress?**

VOLCANO

Notes

Reflection/Ideas/Discussion

WHAT SCENE DURING THIS SESSION STRIKES YOU THE MOST AND WHY?

17. Scene analysis: Looting. There may be nothing more indicative of our culture than the looting which occurs during catastrophes. What are the reasons why people want to loot?
18. Scene analysis: Mike and Dr. Colder try to help the people trapped in the firetruck and those in the street. In general, do you believe that people are helpful to others in times of need? Yes or no and why?
19. Scene analysis: A fireman gives up his life trying to help another. The radio reporter called it "incredible bravery." Where do you see incredible bravery in today's world?
20. Scene analysis: Mike directs Dr. Colder to take Kelly to the hospital. Given the fact that Mike may die, do you think it was the right thing for Mike to do? Yes or no and why?
21. Scene analysis: Kelly tells Dr. Colder that the person they are taking to the hospital is going to die if someone doesn't do something. Obviously, Kelly must begin to "think as an adult" all of a sudden. Do you think that most teenagers can bring themselves to think as adults? Yes or no and why?
22. Dialogue analysis: Mike tells Amy that he cannot just leave the city. In general, do most people show this much responsibility to their jobs? Yes or no and why?
23. Scene analysis: Mike and Amy save a man with the help of the firetruck's ladder apparatus. Obviously an exciting scene, it shows the care we should have for any human being. In general, do most people have respect for the individual lives of human beings? Yes or no and why?

VOLCANO

> 24. **Dialogue/scene analysis**: The policeman and the black man who is complaining that the firetrucks will not go to his house. Who is right and who is wrong during this interchange?
> 25. **Scene analysis**: Mike takes the time to call his daughter. In general, do fathers should as much concern for their daughters as they should? Yes or no and why?
> 26. **Character analysis**: Stan who saved the metro driver, and gave up his life in the process. Obviously, he is a person of prayer as can be seen from the movie. Do you think that there is a connection between bravery and being a person of prayer? Yes or no and why?

Notes

SESSION III
From: After the men are moving the barricade, and Mike says, "Move over there." (Before the scene at the hospital.)
To: End.
Approximate time: 30 minutes.

Theme: Perhaps the greatest lesson of a tragedy is that every person is important.

Scripture: **John 19:25-27** Jesus is concerned about the people he loves.

Doctrine/Application
[*Catechism of the Catholic Church* reference: numbers 1822-1829]

People obviously are the reason why tragedies are tragedies. The eruption of a volcano on an isolated island is different from the eruption of a volcano in a suburb of Los Angeles because of the number of people involved. In either case, the force of nature being what it is, there will be destruction, and in cities with people, there is death and injury. The life stories of the earthquakes in the Los Angeles area attest to

VOLCANO

such a truth. The fiction of the movie "Volcano" therefore includes the tragedies of death and harm which come with catastrophe. But both in real life and fiction, there are always heroes, people who take love of others to the highest level, and people who refuse to recognize any value distinction among human beings. The movie "Volcano" has any number of heroes who give their lives for others. A child will say at the close of the film, speaking of the way everyone looks after the tragedy has been averted, "They all look the same." Black, white, Oriental, European, or American, with the stains of tragedy all over them, people indeed do look the same.

It is love which is the basis for such a contention, of course. True love of others implies a certain willingness to assist one another in a tragedy. In particular, it implies a desire to care for loved ones and friends. Such a scenario of care was seen on a hill outside of Jerusalem at the beginning of the Christian era. During it, the person who was wrongfully accused and brutally punished, in the very throes of immense physical pain, insures that his mother and friend will care for each other. His statement has come down through the years to mean that every Christian not only has a new mother in faith, but indeed, that they are related to one another as "sons and daughters" of that mother. (John 16:25-27)

It has been said that loving others during a tragedy is much easier than loving them in the daily sphere of things. Whether it is true or not, we *do* see immense courage portrayed as people interact during the movie "Volcano." Perhaps the lesson that must also be true however, is that everyone of us must learn to have such love for each other during times when there is no calamity.

Preliminary Thoughts

27. What is your definition of a "hero"?
28. What are the advantages of having Mary the mother of Jesus, as "our mother"?
29. What is most difficult about "love of others" for young people today? Why?

Notes

VOLCANO

Reflection/Ideas/Discussion

WHAT SCENE DURING THIS SESSION STRIKES YOU THE MOST AND WHY?

30. Scene analysis: The television reporter talking of the veterinarian's work during the tragedy. a) Do you believe that we put too much emphasis on animals in our society? b) In particular, do people tend to love their pets more than other human beings?

31. Scene analysis: The policeman and black man reconcile. Often in life, reconciliation such as this is not as easy as it is portrayed in the movie. In general, why is reconciliation so difficult?

32. Scene analysis: Norman and Dr. Jaye Colder's relationship which falls apart during the crisis. a) One has the feeling that this relationship should never have developed. Do you agree and why or why not? b) Do you think that there are many "truly selfish" people like Norman Colder in the world today? Yes or no and why?

33. Dialogue analysis: Amy quotes Matthew's Gospel, chapter 7, verse 26: "And everyone who listens to these words of mine but does not act on them will be like a fool who built his house on sand." It is obvious why Amy said it. What is the principal application of the verse in real life?

34. Dialogue/scene analysis: Thinking that the lava will destroy the hospital, the people talk of trying to "save some." Granted that it is an awful choice, but if the choice had to be made in such an instance, what would you do?

35. Dialogue analysis: Kelly says that the little boy is her *responsibility*. Obviously, she has matured greatly during the tragedy. a) What is the principal responsibility of a young adult in high school in today's world? b) What is the principal responsibility of a young adult in college?

36. Scene analysis: The worker stays with his fellow-worker who is trapped under the column. This was the topic of the meditation for the last session of the movie. Speaking of this scene in particular, was it a good decision? Yes or no and why?

37. Dialogue analysis: As he is looking for his mother, the young child says "They all look the same." It is in part also the topic of the meditation for this session. What is the basis for prejudice against other people?

VOLCANO

> 38. Considering events such as the Oklahoma City bombing and the San Francisco earthquakes, tragedies such as the one portrayed in "Volcano" are quite possible. What does the movie "Volcano" teach concerning tragedies which occur unexpectedly?

Further Material

VOLCANO

INDEX OF SCRIPTURE PASSAGES

Hebrew Scriptures (Old Testament)

Genesis 1:28-31	132
Genesis 2:1-4	63
Genesis 2:18-24	137
Genesis 11:1-9	66
Genesis 24:63-67	71
1 Samuel 20:41-42	142
Psalm 50:15-19	114
Psalm 139:1-18	40

Christian Scriptures (New Testament)

Matthew 2:13-15	160
Matthew 2:19-23	15, 81
Matthew 5:21-22	74
Matthew 5:33-37	101
Matthew 5:38-42	94
Matthew 7:12-14	19
Matthew 12:43-45	24
Matthew 12:46-50	84
Matthew 16:1-4	157
Matthew 19:23-26	104
Matthew 20:17-19	43
Matthew 20:20-22	120
Mark 14:10-11	117
Luke 1:76-79	111
Luke 7:36-50	86
Luke 8:49-55	89
Luke 11:24-26	127
Luke 22:39-46	106
Luke 22:47-53	37

INDEX OF SCRIPTURE PASSAGES

Luke 24:25-27 68

John 7:45-52 .... 92, 140
John 8:31-36 60
John 8:31-38 49
John 10:11-15 150
John 19:4-11 21
John 19:25-27 162

Acts 4:18-21 130
Acts 9:10-17 153
Acts 15:6-12 13
Acts 15:36-41 56
Acts 17:22-28 31

Romans 13:8-10 96

1 Corinthians 7:21-24 77

2 Corinthians 5:6-10 46

Ephesians 6:1-4 122

Colossians 1:21-23 26

James 3:2b-5 34
James 3:2b-10 147

1 Peter 5:8-11 109

1 John 4:11-16 53

INDEX OF THEMES

CARE FOR OTHERS

> Care and concern for another human person is one of the marks of love. *THE SPITFIRE GRILL,* Session II 150

> Communication with each other is the single most important preparation for understanding each other. *CONTACT,* Session II 34

> Even with the most advanced technology, people remain the most important creation. *JURASSIC PARK,* Session III 68

> Helping someone else involves more than simply talking about it. *DEAD MAN WALKING,* Session I 53

> If human beings are governed only by what they want, they will have no respect for animal, man or God. *THE LOST WORLD,* General 127

> In a true friendship, there can be no room for selfishness. *THE MAN WITHOUT A FACE,* Session III 142

> In life, there will be tragedy, and we must learn to work with it, always keeping the importance of people in mind. *VOLCANO,* General 157

> People are more important than law. *SLEEPERS,* Session IV 96

> People can lead fulfilled lives if they feel loved. *SHINE,* Session III 86

> Perhaps the greatest lesson of a tragedy is that every person is important. *VOLCANO,* Session III 162

COMMITMENT

> Often decisions that follow from correct convictions are controversial, and the one who makes them will lose friends. *DEAD MAN WALKING,* Session II 56

CONVERSION

> There can be true conversion only when a person begins to accept responsibility. *DEAD MAN WALKING,* General 53

INDEX OF THEMES

COURAGE

> The courageous person always considers the lives of others no matter what the circumstances. *AIR FORCE ONE,* Session III 26
> We must be courageous, even in the face of severe difficulties. *SPEED 2: CRUISE CONTROL,* General 101

DATING AND MARRIAGE

> First love may be one of the strongest emotions young people ever feel. *ROMEO AND JULIET,* Session I 71
> Learning how to communicate is the most difficult part of preparing for marriage. *SPEED 2: CRUISE CONTROL,* Session I 101
> Passionate love can take away our reason. *ROMEO AND JULIET,* Session III 77

EVIL AT WORK

> Acting in a rage often leads to doing things that we never really want to do. *ROMEO AND JULIET,* Session II 74
> Evil is defined differently depending on one's point of view. But it is always wrong. *AIR FORCE ONE,* Session I 21
> Gossip is one of the great evils among people. *THE SPITFIRE GRILL,* Session I 147
> Greed can cause sickness in a person to such a degree that the person ceases caring for anyone or anything. *SPEED 2: CRUISE CONTROL,* Session II 103
> Love present between two young people in families that hate one another often leads to a tragic end. *ROMEO AND JULIET,* General 71
> Often evil desires drive people more than good desires. *THE LOST WORLD,* Session I 127
> We should have the utmost respect for nature, but our greed often does violence to it. *THE LOST WORLD,* Session III 132
> Prejudice can cease only when we truly understand others and their situations. *A FAMILY THING,* Session I 13
> Religious fanaticism is not the same as religion. *CONTACT,* Session III .. 37

INDEX OF THEMES

EVIL AT WORK, cont.

> Revenge is extremely difficult to control, and when it is done with premeditation, it may affect the people involved forever. *SLEEPERS,* Session III.... 94

> The evil in our world never rests, and therefore we must always fight it. *STAR TREK: FIRST CONTACT,* Session I 109

> When evil controls a situation, evil begets more evil and innocent people always get hurt. *AIR FORCE ONE,* Session II... 24

> When someone suffers a devastating evil because of someone else, the feeling of human nature is toward revenge. *SLEEPERS,* Session II............................. 91

GOD'S PRESENCE IN OUR LIVES

> Even though we can never control all of the tragedies that happen, we must be courageous in our approach to life, accepting what happens. *SPEED 2: CRUISE CONTROL,* Session III 106

> God is often misunderstood because we do not understand God. *CONTACT,* Session I 31

> God is with us, no matter how we think. *CONTACT,* Session IV 40

FAMILY

> A parent who has deep-seated mental problems will always influence the family in a negative way. *THE GREAT SANTINI,* General 117

> In order to feel satisfied in life, one must truly understand one's immediate family. *A FAMILY THING,* Session II... 15

> Family members can be friends with each other only when they are giving to each other. *A FAMILY THING,* Session III... 18

> Parents will always influence their children. *THE GREAT SANTINI,* Session III 122

> The circumstances in which a child grows up including family and neighborhood affect that child's life forever. *SLEEPERS,* Session I................. 89

> The influence of a father on a growing person is enormous. *SHINE,* Session I 81

INDEX OF THEMES

FRIENDSHIP

> The gift of trust and love is the greatest gift a friend can give another. *THE MAN WITHOUT A FACE,* General 137
> True friendship involves the true sharing of ideals and ideas. *THE MAN WITHOUT A FACE,* Session II 140

IMPROVING LIFE

> Admitting the truth always enables one to live and die well. *DEAD MAN WALKING,* Session III 59
> In order to know people completely, we have to comprehend why they act the way they do. *THE SPITFIRE GRILL,* General 147
> Peace can be achieved when people finally work together. *STAR TREK: FIRST CONTACT,* Session II 111
> People do not read signs of impending danger very well. *VOLCANO,* Session I 157
> The greatest thing that we can offer ourselves or others is the truth. *COURAGE UNDER FIRE,* General 43
> Science and technology should teach us that we are not alone in our universe because there is a Higher Power who has created it. *CONTACT,* General 31
> The results of our incredible technology must be regulated by the principles of God and not by the world. *JURASSIC PARK,* Session I 63
> The truth will always set us free. *COURAGE UNDER FIRE,* Session III. 49
> We cannot live by ourselves all our lives; we need other people. *THE MAN WITHOUT A FACE,* Session I 137

INTEGRITY OF CHARACTER

> Before we make decisions concerning a person, we must know that person well. *THE SPITFIRE GRILL,* Session III 153
> Good deeds often end up hurting the people who bring them about. *THE LOST WORLD,* Session II 129
> Sometimes doing the right thing means giving everything we have. *STAR TREK: FIRST CONTACT,* General 109

INDEX OF THEMES

INTEGRITY OF CHARACTER, cont.

> When we know the truth, we can never really hide it. *COURAGE UNDER FIRE,* Session II 46

MATURITY

> An important part of maturity is getting to know one's family. *A FAMILY THING,* General 13

> In times of stress, people must act in a mature manner. *VOLCANO,* Session II 159

> Much of the time, adults are the way they are because of their early lives. *SHINE,* General 81

> Sometimes our decisions cause consequences that affect us deeply. *COURAGE UNDER FIRE,* Session I 43

> The wounds of childhood not only carry through life, but they direct our actions unless we control them. *SLEEPERS,* General 89

> When we understand the idea of sacrifice, we will understand what maturity is. *STAR TREK: FIRST CONTACT,* Session III 114

> Young people must find their own way at some time in their lives. *SHINE,* Session II 84

PROBLEMS IN LIFE

> As long as people believe in a cause, they can do harm unless they are ruled by morally correct principles. *AIR FORCE ONE,* General 21

> People who work with unknown powers often end up hurting themselves and others. *JURASSIC PARK,* General 63

> People with strong personalities often make it difficult on themselves and on others. *THE GREAT SANTINI,* Session I 117

INDEX OF THEMES

SELFISHNESS

> We cannot live our lives vicariously through someone close to us. *THE GREAT SANTINI,* Session II 120

> When our technology is not regulated by the principles of God, selfishness takes over. *JURASSIC PARK,* Session II 66